> *Looking for an opportunity in 2025, please get educated on **live social shopping**.*

GARY VAYNERCHUK
Industry thought leader and live seller

YOUR **LIVE SELLING** LAUNCHPAD

GO [LIVE] & thrive

Start your livestream shopping business and earn your first sales in just 21 days

Olivia Chen

OLIVIA CHEN PRESENTS
GO LIVE & THRIVE - YOUR LIVE SELLING LAUNCHPAD

Copyright © 2025 Sterling Press. All rights reserved.

This book of any portion thereof may not be reproduced, stored in a retrieval system, or transmitted, in any form or by any means, electronic, mechanical, photocopying. recording or distributing any part of it in any form without prior written permission from the publisher.

Printed locally
0921 002
2 4 6 8 10 9 7 5 3

First Edition, May 2025

Paperback ISBN: 978-3-98552-337-5

Disclaimer: The information contained within this book is for educational and entertainment purposes only. All effort has been executed to present up to date, accurate, reliable, complete information. No warranties or guaranteed earnings of any kind are declared or implied. Readers acknowledge that the author is not engaged in the rendering of legal, financial, medical or professional advice. The content within this book has been derived from various sources. Any brands or tools mentioned are not endorsements, nor are they affiliated in any way with the author or the publisher.

Sterling Press, Torbrex, Stirling, FK7 9HD, United Kingdom
For enquiries, please email spbookcomms@gmail.com

Editorial
Director **Jacqueline Chang**

Production
Project Manager **Richard Walker**

Illustrations
Arthub, Macrovector, Dena Yune

Cover
Tar Zhanova

All copyrights and trademarks are recognized and respected

DEDICATION

This book is dedicated to the people who lifted me up, believed in me and occasionally reminded me to fix my lighting before going live!

To my grandmother, who taught me patience and the value of hard work, and to my mother, who always told me that passion and business could go hand in hand. To my father, who showed me that obstacles are just stepping stones (even when I tripped over them) and to my friends, who sat through far too many test runs and cheered me on through every nervous attempt.

And to my best friend. You know this book wouldn't exist without all the times you made me laugh so hard I completely forgot I was supposed to be selling something. If the time you shouted **THAT'S A BLOOPER!** in the background two seconds after I knocked my camera off the tripod and disappeared mid-stream has taught me anything, it's that nothing beats authenticity with a little chaos.

Finally, to the incredible community of live sellers who welcomed me, shared wisdom and reminded me that showing up as yourself is the best strategy of all. This book is for all of you.

MY STORY

Hey there, I'm Olivia Chen, a creative introvert who found her voice live streaming about fashion on Douyin. When my family moved to America, it rocked my confidence, and that old shyness found its way back into my life. I had to learn to feel brave all over again. So, I turned back to live streaming, sharing my life and love for clothes. I then took a leap and opened a TikTok Shop selling women's casualwear. In just three weeks, I was making over $1,000 in revenue in a single stream. But I don't do it for the money. I do it to have fun and be true with my audience. I even add little quirks to my streams, like ironing live on camera, because why the heck not, right? And you can succeed too. Just lean in on the advice in this book and start your own journey.

Full disclosure, I'm using my name for this book, not my social handle. Why? Well, it wasn't an easy decision. Sure, I'd benefit from revealing my brand, like more visibility and getting more viewers. But I prefer to keep a clear boundary between the content in this book and my brand as a live seller. It lets me be more mindful about crafting my personal and online identities. More importantly, I'd feel terrible if my lovely regular viewers were to misinterpret my advice on sales techniques in this book as insincere or deceptive. And that's simply not the case because I truly care about my audience and maintaining the trust and respect we've built together.

Your only limit is you

WHY YOU NEED THIS BOOK

I assume you picked up this book because you:

- want to understand the ins-and-outs of the fastest-growing ecommerce trend.

- are a content creator.

- have already established a following or fan base.
  (If you haven't already, focus on building your audience first.)

- have a budget for livestreaming equipment, product samples and inventory.

- want a simple, stress-free guide to get started with live selling.

- are a visual learner who learns better with pictures and graphics rather than walls of text.

- don't have time to attend expensive online courses.

- know that what's easy to do is also easy not to do. Commit to following each bite-sized step in this book.

- want the flexibility to work from anywhere, even on vacation.

- want to be your own boss and have control of your career.

WHY 21 DAYS

QUICK WINS

You're excited to get started. I get that. I was too. This book takes your initial excitement and turns it into action. That's why there's a lot to for you to learn and do on the first few days. It's all about helping you hit the ground running. So, dive in, start strong and make the most of your eagerness.

HELLO, BIG MO

Each day's success builds on the previous one, creating a positive cycle that keeps you motivated. And the more you stick to it, the more momentum you build. That's when "Big Mo" steps in and starts rewarding you for your continued efforts with even greater success.

TIPS & SHORTCUTS
You'll find handy tips sprinkled throughout the book.

 Simple, practical advice that can be easily applied right away.

 Advanced techniques for achieving expert-level results.

WEEKENDS OFF

I know you have other stuff to do and people you wanna spend time with. That's why the days you invest in this don't have to be in a row. Just do what you can on days that you can. Some of you may be learning on weekends around your normal 9-5 job. Others will learn workdays and take weekends off (like me most weekends chilling with my cockapoo cutey, Angus). Either way, you'll be a pro in no time!

LET'S CONNECT

Would you like to connect with me and other live sellers in a Skool community where we swap tips and give each other support? I haven't set it up yet, but if you'd like to hear about it if I do, send me an empty email with "Skool" as the subject. I promise I won't spam you or try to sell you anything.

I'm at: **oliviachenlive@gmail.com**

CONTENTS

IT AIN'T YOUR GRANDMA'S QVC!
Get the basics of live selling and see how brands and influencers across the world are making real-time shopping feel fresh and approachable.

PAGES: 12-21

GEARING UP FOR THE JOURNEY
Lay the groundwork by combining great equipment, the right platform, a sharp niche, quality products, a strong brand, and a USP that makes you unforgettable.

DAYS: 1-5 | PAGES: 22-69

PREPPING FOR THE SPOTLIGHT
It's almost time to shine. Map out your show's timeline, ease your camera jitters, prepare for tech hiccups and create buzz for your upcoming live selling debut.

DAYS: 6-10 | PAGES: 70-103

GOING LIVE
Check off your pre-show essentials and then rock your first live selling event with genuine energy. Wrap up by reflecting on your performance to keep getting better.

DAY: 11 | PAGES: 104-113

SHIP ORDERS & ANALYSIS

Wrap up your show by making sure orders and returns are handled smoothly, then take a moment to reflect on the experience and uncover some fresh ideas for next time.

DAYS: 12-13 | PAGES: 114-127

SCALING YOUR OPERATIONS

Build a stronger, more connected brand by merging lively events with streamlined processes and creative partnerships that keep your audience engaged and excited.

DAYS: 14-16 | PAGES: 128-153

PERFECTING YOUR CRAFT

Be unapologetically you, using your natural charm to engage fans, sprinkling in fun attention-grabbers, clever urgency tactics and positive customer shoutouts.

DAYS: 17-20 | PAGES: 154-181

LIGHTS, CAMERA, CHA-CHING!

Bring together all the skills you've learned to create an authentic, entertaining and high-earning live selling event that's fun for you and your viewers.

DAY: 21 | PAGES: 182-191

THE ROAD AHEAD

Where do you go from here? As you map out your future, think about your next milestones, leveling up your equipment and tapping into cool tech trends like AI and AR.

PAGES: 192-205

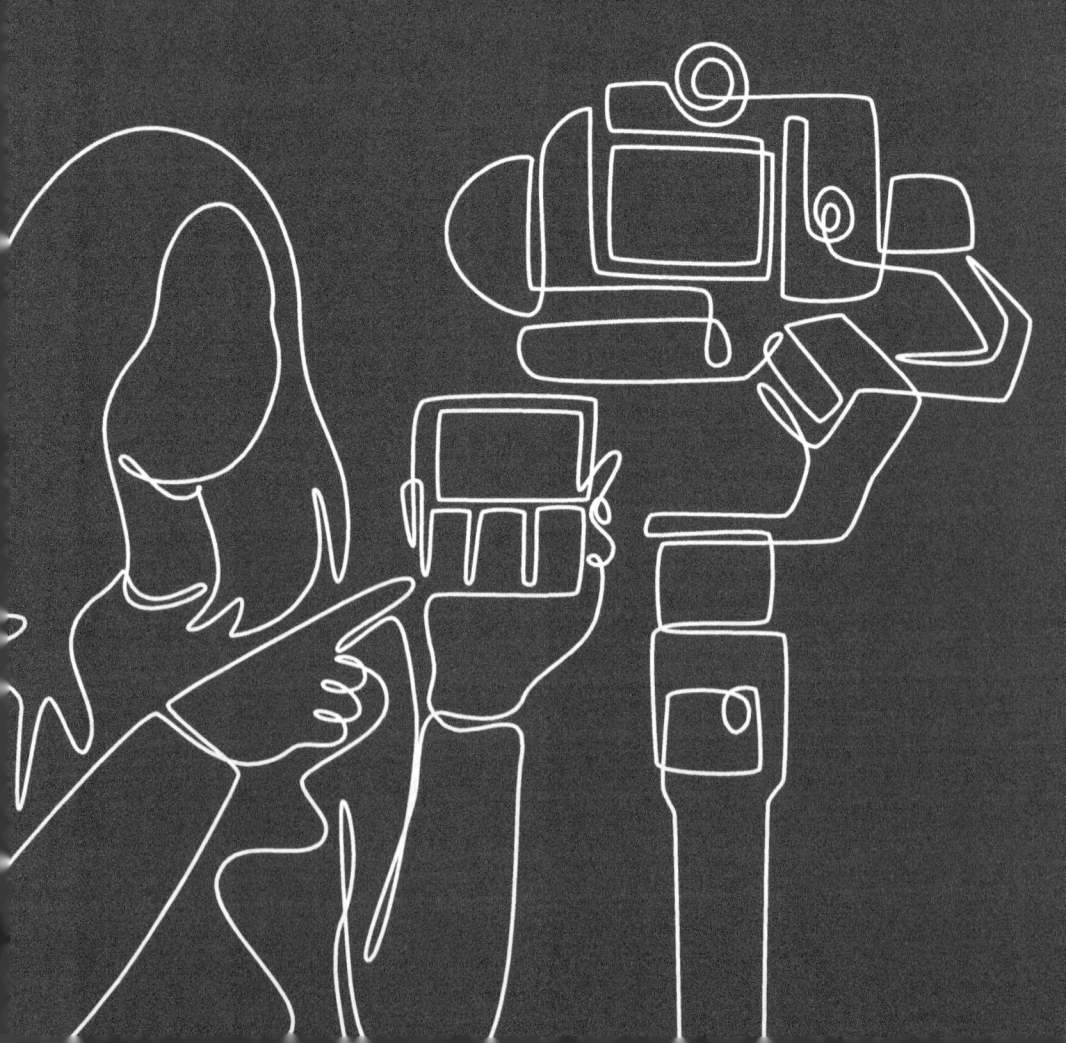

IT AIN'T YOUR GRANDMA'S QVC!

14 | IT AIN'T YOUR GRANDMA'S QVC!

LIVE SELLING
HOW IT WORKS

Blending entertainment with instant checkouts, live selling gives retailers, brands and content creators a new channel to interact with buyers in real time.

No, it's not the future of shopping, it's already here and it's growing fast!

You picked up this book because you want to begin selling live soon. Well, you're in luck. There's never been a better time to get started.

It won't take you long to grasp enough of the basics to get in front of a camera and start having fun with your audience.

> Live selling goes by many names like 'live social shopping', 'livestream selling' and 'live commerce'. I've even heard the term 'shoppertainment'. For this book, I'll stick with 'live selling'. Please take it to mean all those terms.

I guess you already know what live selling is, so I'll spare you the boring details. What I thought would be fun though, is give you some examples of amazing live selling influencers in action that you can use for your own inspiration.

Tune in to their streams if you get the chance.

THE BEAUTY GURU

Beauty guru and makeup artist Carla Stevenne has leveraged her Amazon Live shop to share beauty tips and tricks with her YouTube subscribers and Instagram followers. Her Amazon Live streams, packed with beauty product recommendations, have become a huge hit among her fans.

INTRODUCTION | 15

TRENDY TUNES

Aspiring musician and TikTok sensation Nate Wyatt, with millions of TikTok followers, teamed up with celebrity stylist Mimi Cuttrell for a live shopping event with Aldo. Showcasing spring fashion and style tips, the stream boasted an impressive 308% engagement rate, cementing Wyatt's influence in the live selling world.

THE PIONEER WOMAN

Ree Drummond has charmed her more than 4 million Instagram followers with live shopping events for Walmart. Her popularity as a food writer and TV host made her the perfect ambassador for Walmart's Pioneer Woman Collection, allowing fans to purchase items directly from her lively streams.

MAKING METAL WORK

DIY enthusiast and metalwork aficionado Renaud Bauer shares his passion with tens of thousands of subscribers through his YouTube channel, Renaud Bauer – Createur. His live shopping events for Batimat showcase the latest tools and materials, attracting fellow metalwork lovers and DIY enthusiasts to his cool and informative streams.

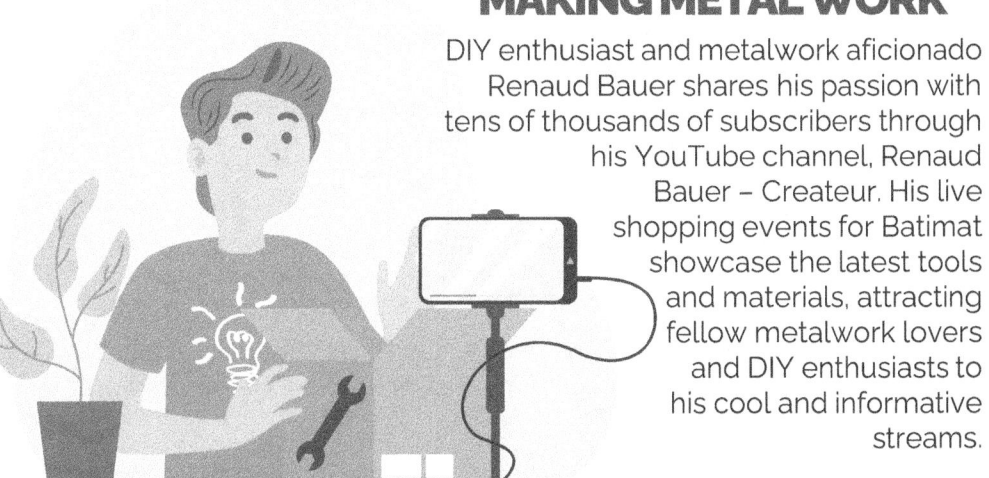

16 | IT AIN'T YOUR GRANDMA'S QVC!

SHOPPING
IN YOUR SLIPPERS

Think of live shopping as the 21st-century version of classic TV shopping networks like QVC and the Home Shopping Network. But, unlike the old model where viewers were tied to their TVs, live selling lets you tune in and shop from virtually anywhere.

THE CORE APPEAL OF HOME SHOPPING

Both TV and social channels involve selling products through live video presentations, but here's how they differ:

LIVE SHOPPING ONLINE

- **Interactivity**: Buyers can ask questions and get instant answers.
- **Accessibility**: Available on various social media platforms.
- **Instant Purchase Options**: Integrated purchase buttons or links during live streams.
- **Engagement Tools**: Use of polls, giveaways and shoutouts.
- **Flexible Schedule**: Streams can happen anytime, anywhere.
- **Personalized Experience**: Targeted content for specific audiences.

LIVE SHOPPING ON TV

- **Scheduled Programs**: Set times for shows and product segments.
- **Accessibility**: For those who might not be online-savvy.
- **Professional Production**: High-quality production with polished hosts and demos.
- **Trust and Credibility**: Established channels and loyal followers.
- **Longer Segments**: Detailed product demonstrations.
- **Customer Service**: Robust support for inquiries and orders.

REINVENTING Home Shopping

On TV, communication only goes one way.

Live sellers engage in real-time.

TV shows run on a very tight schedule.

Livestreams can run for as long as you like, making sure all questions get answered.

Sure, TV viewers do call in, but they're screened. And they vary on each show.

On a live stream, comments come at any time and from many of the same people, so you can build relationships over time.

TV shopping channels usually feature a limited range of hosts.

Live sellers often collaborate with influencers and brand ambassadors, reaching a broader and more diverse audience.

TV shopping relies on phone orders.

Live selling uses instant online purchase options, simplifying the buying process.

18 | IT AIN'T YOUR GRANDMA'S QVC!

EAST vs WEST
FROM CHINA TO THE WORLD

In China, live shopping is already massive, and likely gonna be a trillion-dollar industry very soon, if not already by the time you read this. Influencers are selling out products in minutes on platforms like Taobao Live and Douyin (TikTok). This explosive success hints at what's coming globally.

WHY PEOPLE LOVE LIVE SHOPPING IN CHINA

Many prefer shopping from home rather than going to crowded malls to find what they need, a trend that grew during the lockdowns. No traffic, long lines, social distancing or parking struggles.

Chinese consumers love the educational value of live streams, often buying based on hosts' demos, like "lipstick king" Li Jiaqi (**look him up!**) showing off different shades of red lipstick.

Live selling isn't just useful, it's entertaining. Shopping streams can be like TV shows or movies. They're often hosted by celebs, making them fun and engaging for viewers.

Chinese consumers like the chance to chat in real time with real people about products and get immediate answers, just like in-store shopping.

Chinese consumers are used to shifts in ecommerce trends and almost every person in China shops online using their smartphone.

TOP REASON: Prices during a live selling event are usually cheaper thanks to exclusive discounts, and viewers often have the chance to haggle. Bargain!

INTRODUCTION | 19

BUT DOES IT WORK IN THE WEST?

In 2016, Alibaba shook up shopping with live selling, transforming how people in China shopped online. The West is catching on, with trends shifting towards this fun and interactive way to shop.

China's live commerce boom has sparked copycats. But just copying Chinese sellers isn't enough. To make it work elsewhere, you've got to think about the local culture and what people like to buy and how they shop.

SHOPPING CULTURE

It's said that over 80% of social media users in China shop in the platforms. In the West, on the other hand, most social media users have yet to make a single purchase that way.

Make ordering a breeze for users.
See Day 4.

VIEWING CULTURE

In the West, social media is all about fast, dopamine-filled scrolling on TikTok and Reels. Users just don't wanna spend half an hour on one video.

Find the right platform.
See Day 2.

HOSTING CULTURE

Chinese livestreams really dazzle with dual hosts, slick production and engaging formats, making it a real show. Livestreams in other countries often feel a bit dull, like old-school public access TV.

Master the art of entertaining.
See Day 7.

IT AIN'T YOUR GRANDMA'S QVC!
BIG BRANDS OR
SOLO STARS

Many brands are dipping their toes into the water of live selling. But who you have in front of the camera matters. Some retailers host livestream events their own platform, some collaborate with influencers and others, like you, are content creators not affiliated with any brand and are selling products you believe in.

HOSTING LIVESTREAMS YOURSELF

PROS

YOU DO YOU (AUTHENTIC CONNECTION)
Your audience loves you for you. Hosting your own streams keeps that genuine vibe strong and lets your personality shine.

YOUR RULES (CREATIVE CONTROL)
You decide how to present products in a way that feels true to your style and resonates with your followers.

REAL RECOMMENDATIONS (BUILDING TRUST)
When you genuinely endorse products, your audience trusts your word, boosting engagement and sales.

CONS

ON YOUR SHOULDERS (EXTRA WORKLOAD)
Managing content creation, hosting and product promotion can be a lot to juggle solo.

SOLO EFFORT (LIMITED RESOURCES)
Without a team or brand support, you're up against it in terms of production quality and reach.

INTRODUCTION | 21

As you grow as an influencer, you'll probably start thinking about collaborating with brands and selling their products during your livestreams. Knowing the pros of working with influencers and why retailers might be hesitant to collaborate with you can help you navigate the path to successful brand partnerships.

INFLUENCERS

VS

RETAIL STAFF

GOOD FOR INFLUENCERS
Influencers are pros at keeping viewers glued, it's their superpower. An influencer's charisma can boost a brand's recognition and keep audiences hooked. Partnering with a trusted influencer also means tapping into their loyal fans. These fans can become your brand ambassadors, spreading the word and boosting a brand's reach even further.

Like when Kohl's teamed up with YouTube star Judy Travis of ItsJudyTime for their Black Friday Sale. Her vlog shopping with her mom got around 200,000 views!

YOUR OBSTACLES
Teaming up with influencers can be pricey and doesn't always guarantee results. And if an influencer doesn't vibe with the brand, viewers might see through it and tune out.

GOOD FOR RETAILERS
Staff know the products inside out. By positioning key opinions employees (KOEs) as subject matter experts, they bring authenticity, making viewers more likely to trust and buy from the brand directly. Using already salaried employees instead of influencers means brands can use the money saved for bigger marketing resources, better equipment and promotional boosts.

Sideshow held a live shopping event for its 28th birthday hosted by two team members, featuring exclusive collectibles, flash giveaways and fun promos.

YOUR OPPORTUNITIES
Starting without an influencer means a lot less viewers at first, so it'll take more time for a brand to build an audience. Plus, not all staff are naturals on camera, meaning time and money spent on training.

GEARING UP FOR THE JOURNEY

24 | GEARING UP FOR THE JOURNEY
DAY 1: SETTING UP
YOUR STAGE

Start with the background. A solid-colored wall or green screen works best. You can even personalize the background with your branding.

You don't need a huge space to turn into a studio. A cozy corner in your home works just fine.

You'll need a table to easily grab products, props and devices you need for your streams.

THE PERFECT SINGLE-CAM SETUP

A simple single-camera setup is an excellent option for starting out without making a large financial commitment. As you get more comfortable with streaming, you can gradually add equipment.

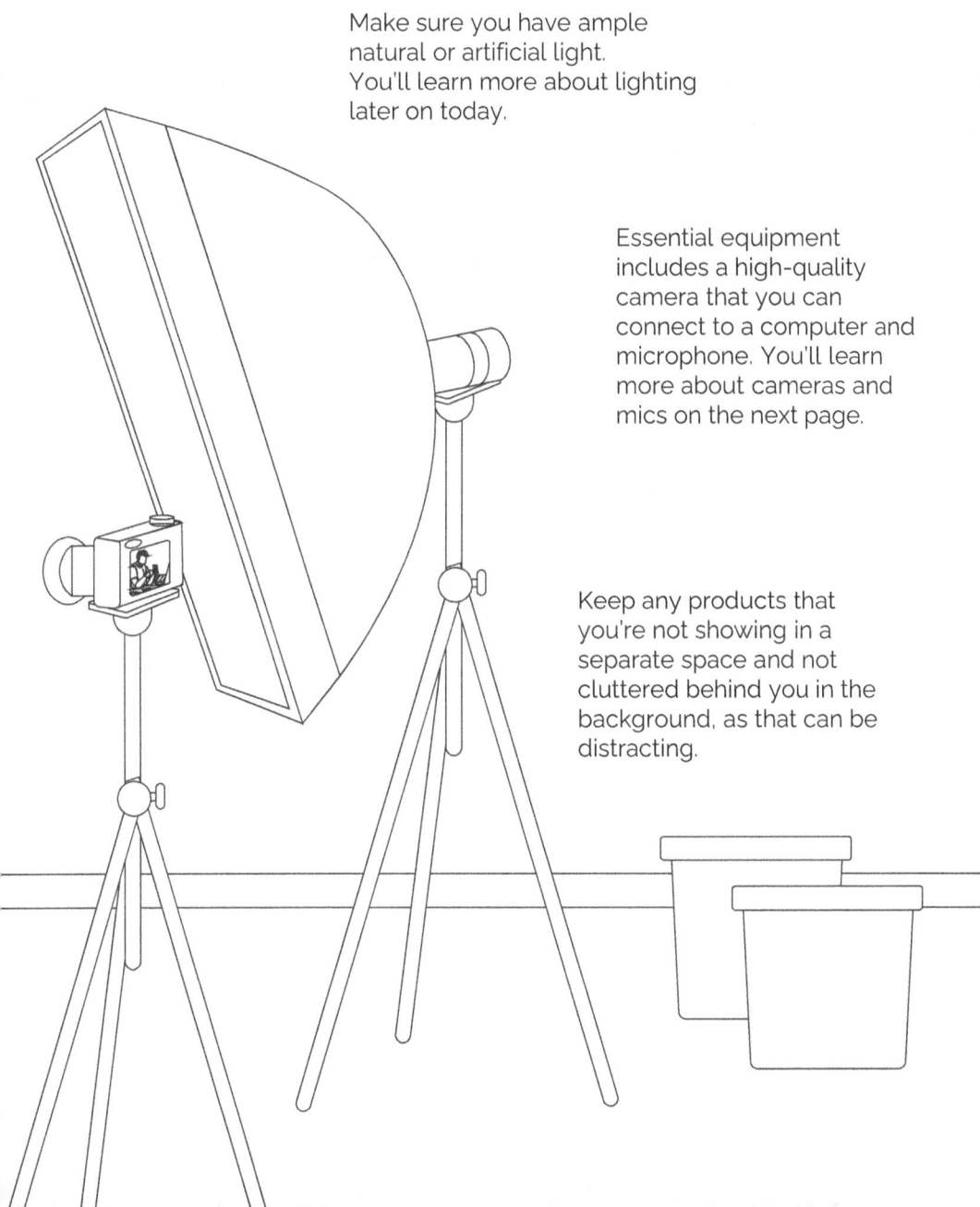

Make sure you have ample natural or artificial light. You'll learn more about lighting later on today.

Essential equipment includes a high-quality camera that you can connect to a computer and microphone. You'll learn more about cameras and mics on the next page.

Keep any products that you're not showing in a separate space and not cluttered behind you in the background, as that can be distracting.

DAY 1: THE ESSENTIAL EQUIPMENT

BASICS YOU CAN'T STREAM WITHOUT

  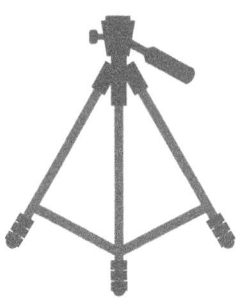

SMARTPHONE

Smartphones are fantastic for live selling because they're so easy to use and already have the features you need to get started. But mainly, they're great because you've already got one!

Smartphone video and audio quality gets better all the time. They're also portable, so you can stream from anywhere and keep things fun and flexible. It's everything you need to go live in one handy package!

VIDEO CAMERA

For live selling, a video camera is simply the better choice over a smartphone for far greater flexibility and performance. There are so many camcorders out there to suit all budgets but aim for one that offers 4K video, XLR audio input and SDI output. With 4K video, your streams will be crisp and detailed, XLR audio inputs let you to connect an external mic for clear and immersive sound, while SDI outputs give you a reliable way to connect to your external systems.

TRIPOD/MOUNT

A tripod (or a table mount) is one of the best tools you can add to your setup. It keeps your camera steady and can double up as a stand for your lights. If you're running the show solo, having a tripod for your camera is crucial.

Nobody enjoys shaky footage. It breaks the flow and makes it harder for viewers to stay engaged.

GO LIVE & THRIVE - DAY 1 | **27**

LOOKING GOOD AND LOOKING BETTER!
I haven't listed it here, but good lighting is another non-negotiable for live selling. You'll look better if you use an external light source instead of your device's built-in light. But it doesn't have to cost a lot. Read on for a deep dive into lighting and how to nail your setup.

MICROPHONE

COMPUTER

FAST INTERNET

Smartphones can record audio but they're terrible for making you sound echoey and picking up noises like wind or traffic.

So, you basically have two choices: A lavalier mic is small, discreet and clips onto your clothes. That means you can move around your space freely while showcasing products. A shotgun mic is your best bet for professional audio, reducing background noise and echoes, but you'll have to stay in the same spot to use it.

Live selling requires a device, and laptops and desktops tend to perform best. Your smartphone can work, but its wireless connection won't always be steady. Plus, a computer lets you easily connect external mics and webcams.

Make sure your computer has enough processing power for streaming. Connect it to the internet using an ethernet cable for a faster, more reliable connection.

To stream live, you need a fast internet connection; especially with a good upload speed. But what is a good upload speed? Check what your chosen platform recommends and then run a test to see if you're covered.

Be aware that you'll be uploading video *constantly*, so your upload speed needs to be stable too. There's a bunch of online tutorials where you can learn about ideal upload speed and how to optimize it.

DAY 1: SOME OTHER GEAR YOU MIGHT NEED

You'll need a camera and mic of course, but what else? Here's a breakdown of other live streaming equipment.

THE LOW DOWN ON EXTRA STUFF

ADJUSTABLE ARM

Adjustable arms make it easy to position your mic just right for clear sound, with quick and quiet mic adjustments during your live streams. They also free up desk space because they're attached to just the edge. And, let's be honest, they look cool.

It's a smart upgrade for your audio setup but not essential. Many studio arms can even hold a pop shield, if you have one.

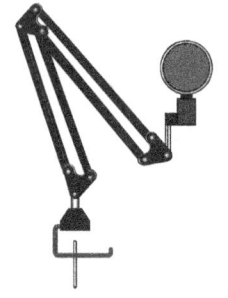

POP SHIELD

Pop shields block those pesky puffs of air "pops" from hitting your mic as you speak, making you sound natural and clear.

Place it between your mouth and your mic, and it acts as a barrier against unwanted pops, hisses and plosive sounds like 'p' and 'b'. You know the ones that are really distracting and annoying when you're watching something.

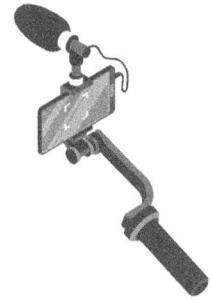

GIMBAL

A gimbal is a tool for live streaming on the move. It's perfect if you're walking around your studio (behind-the-scenes) and shooting outdoors.

It lets you smoothly pan, tilt and track your movements while keeping your footage steady (you don't want viewers feeling seasick from watching you).

Note that they need energy to work, so go for a model with good battery life.

INVEST WHAT YOU CAN AFFORD, NEVER MORE!

Being a good live seller is about capturing your viewer's attention; not how expensive your equipment is. Here's your challenge: Go live for the first few months without spending more than $100 on equipment.

GREEN SCREEN

With a green screen, you can replace your background with live-motion videos, photos and Hollywood-style effects using editing software. This lets you brand your live streams and gives you options to present different backgrounds when the need arises.

Keep in mind that green screens work best when they're wrinkle free and evenly lit. And don't wear green, unless you're going for a disembodied head look!

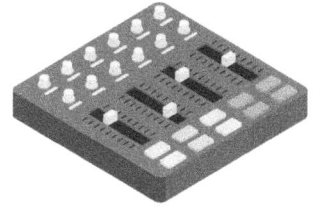

AUDIO MIXER

An audio mixer is used to mix, balance, combine and adjust the volumes of multiple sources of audio into one signal.

You'll really only need one if you regularly use more than one mic, play music or broadcast videos on your streams. And I recommend it for leveling up your game later, not when you're starting out.

VIDEO SWITCHER

If you're using multiple cameras for your live streams, a video switcher lets you easily switch between them. You're simply choosing which feed to send live at any given moment, whether it's a different camera angle, recorded video, slide deck or other graphics.

Both hardware and software switchers can be great options but not something to invest in for single-camera setups.

DAY 1: A BEGINNER'S GUIDE TO LIGHTING

Key lights, fill lights, back lights, natural light, ring lights. Lighting can seem daunting at first, but it's simpler than you might think.

Unlike our eyes, cameras don't process light the same way, so you need a well-lit set to make your on-screen image look natural. But, grabbing every lamp you have and pointing them at your face isn't the answer. Sure, more light can make things better, but only if you set it up correctly.

Live streaming works well with a three-point lighting system, using three different types of lights for your videos:

- **Key light**: The main light source (natural light can be used instead).
- **Fill light**: "Fills" in shadows created by the key light.
- **Back light**: Separates you from the background.

You can learn more about each of these lights across the page. The major downside of the three-point lighting system is just how freaking expensive it is. Not only do you need to buy the lights, but also stands to put the lights on as well as a diffuser to soften and spread the light from your key light.

On the bright side (ha!), you don't need all those lights if you use a **ring light**. Many experienced streamers use them because they're easier to set up, cheaper and they make the set look just as good.

PRO HACK

Glasses cause glare (this holds especially true for ring lights), and it's very distracting to viewers. If you wear glasses when live streaming, play around with your shooting angle, soften your light source, add lights and try tilting your glasses, so your viewers can see your face without a reflection.

KEY LIGHT
(MAIN LIGHT)

The key light serves as your main light source. It's typically the brightest and most influential light in your setup. It's placed at eye level and slightly to one side in front of you (45 degrees is ideal).

NATURAL LIGHT

Natural lighting can be your best friend or worst enemy. It's free and your skin will look natural. But cloudy days make it dark and direct sunlight is too intense. It's an option if you have big windows and stream during daylight hours.

RING LIGHT
(ALL-IN-ONE)

LED ring lights need almost zero set up, are easier to use and take up a lot less space compared to a 3-point lighting setup. They also cost a heck of a lot less.

BACK LIGHT
(FOR DEPTH)

The backlight sits behind you, separating you from the background and creating a sharper outline. It's usually angled on the same side as the key light, directly opposite it. You can see what I mean on the next page.

FILL LIGHT
(FOR BALANCE)

Fill lights help get rid of shadows that your key light misses and creates. They sit opposite the key light and should be set at 50-75% of the key light's strength. Umbrellas and softboxes both work well as fill lights.

DAY 1: LIGHTING YOUR STAGE

Good lighting makes all the difference for live streaming. It can boost quality or become a distraction. Here are six typical lighting setups to help you find one that works for you.

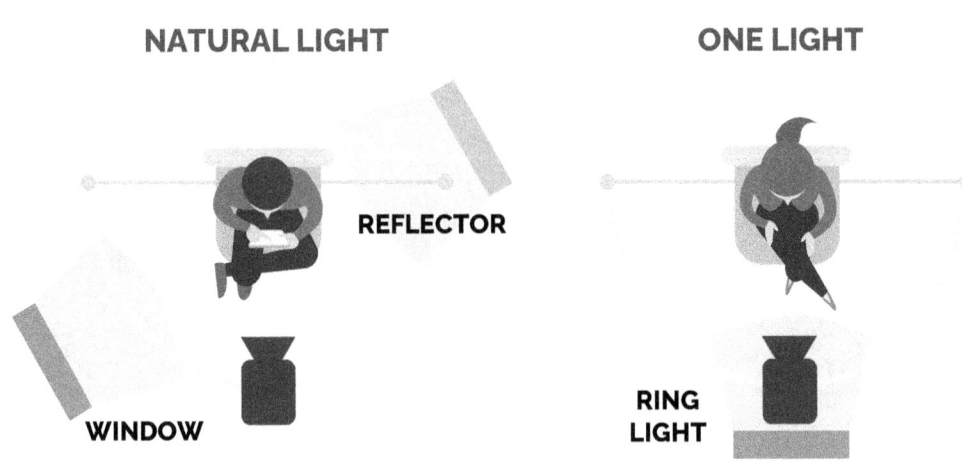

NATURAL LIGHT

Natural lighting is the best, and obviously the cheapest! If you're filming near a window, have the light in front of you, not behind, and sit a little to the side. Make the most of your window lighting by adding a reflector on the other side directly opposite the window. Voila, natural loop lighting!

ONE LIGHT

For a single-light setup, a ring light is an excellent choice. Position it directly behind your camera to create even, balanced lighting that highlights your face and minimizes shadows. It's an efficient way to elevate your video quality with minimal effort, minimal expense and minimal space.

LOOP LIGHTING

TWO LIGHTS

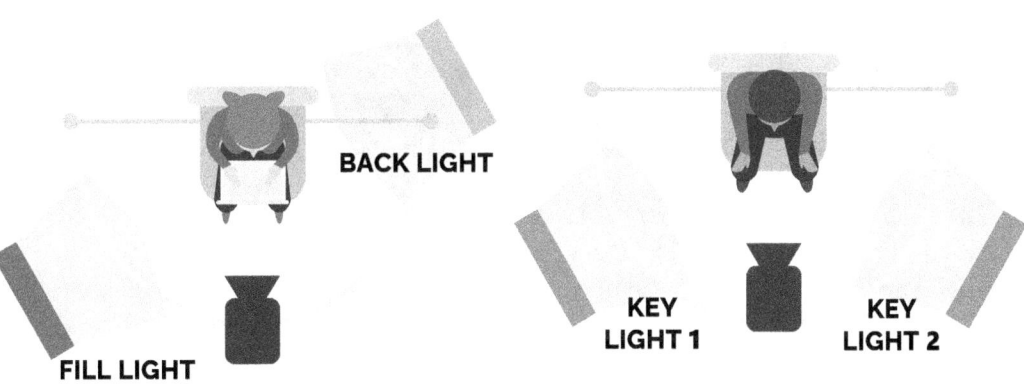

To achieve loop lighting, position the key light to the side of your camera, slightly above eye level. Place the fill light on the opposite side to reduce shadows. It's a versatile improvement over a ring light, providing better depth and minimizing uneven lighting.

Using two key lights on either side of your camera is great for clear and polished visuals. It's also super easy to set up and great for direct shots, but it can make your videos appear flat and lack depth.

3-POINT LIGHTING

FOUR LIGHTS

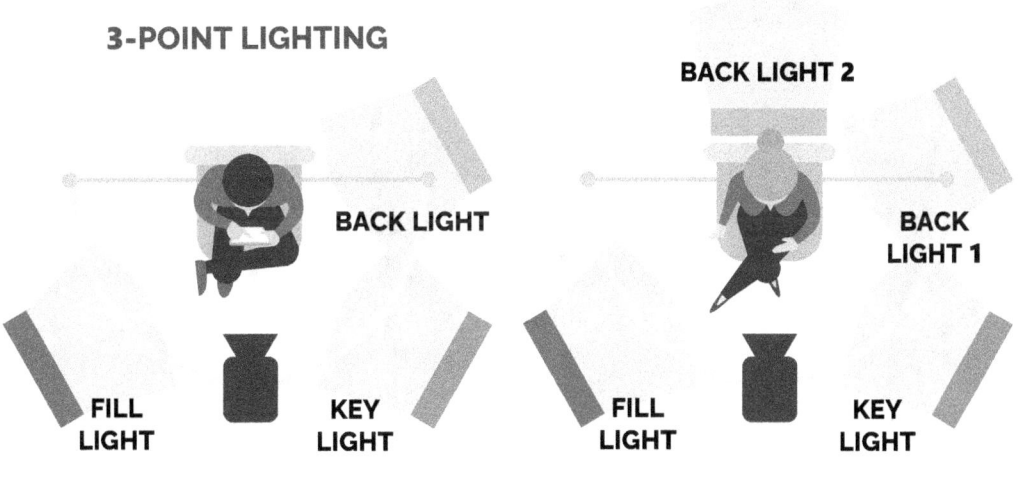

Three-point lighting, with a key light, fill light and backlight, is the setup of choice for streamers and YouTubers for clear, professional visuals. It creates a 3D look, evenly lighting you from all angles. Another favorite is to add a diffuser to the backlight for a softer, more natural glow.

You can enhance your three-point lighting by adding a background light, positioned waist-high behind you to brighten the backdrop and eliminate unwanted shadows for a cleaner look. This won't work for all backgrounds, and of course, it's the most expensive and cumbersome.

34 | GEARING UP FOR THE JOURNEY
DAY 2: PICKING YOUR
PLATFORM

Time to pick your platform. This is the place where you'll go live on air. Discoverability is key, so start by identifying where the audience for your products hangs out. If your research says they're on YouTube, then that's your go-to for live streaming.

TOP PLATFORMS (not an endorsement!)
Availability depends on where you live.

YOUTUBE LIVE

More than silly cat videos, YouTube is a powerhouse for creators and brands, offering real-time interaction with a massive audience. You can even monetize your live videos.

Eligible channels enjoy extra features like product tagging, promo codes and video overlays that allow shoppers to buy products while keeping your video on their smartphone screen.

Must-knows:
- Only open to members of the YouTube Partner Program.

TIKTOK SHOP

TikTok is massive with a younger crowd and most watch over an hour of videos every day.

TikTok Shop lets you sell products directly through your videos, with about 35% of users saying they bought something on the platform. And it's free to get started as TikTok charges commission fees on purchases.

Must-knows:
- While it's easy to set up, the real challenge lies in standing out. Be prepared to create engaging content daily.

AMAZON LIVE

If you sell on Amazon, or plan to, Amazon's got a built-in live shopping platform. Use the Amazon Live Creator app to make and manage your streams. Your products show up next to the video, and deals pop up in the carousel.

Amazon's huge customer base means more potential buyers compared to other platforms, and you could get your stream to appear on multiple places like the website, Prime Video and Amazon Freevee.

Must-knows:
- Only open to registered sellers and in certain countries.

WHATNOT

As a full-service live selling platform, Whatnot has a bunch of useful features not found on other platforms.

The live auction format is worth pointing out as it can lead to quicker sales compared to traditional listings by creating a sense of urgency and gamification among viewers.

Must-knows:
- Like auctions on eBay, you could end up selling an item much lower than you wanted to.

MORE LIVE SELLING PLATFORMS TO DIG INTO

Some of these stream on their own platform, while others let you broadcast from your website and/or across your social media channels.

Poshmark	eBay Live
Firework	GoLive
Livescale	Popshop Live
Bambuser	TalkShopLive
CommentSold	Confer With
Channelize.io	BuyItLive

WHAT ABOUT FACEBOOK AND INSTAGRAM?
Meta stopped live selling in 2022 (they'll come to their senses!). Technically, you can still host live shopping events on these platforms by using another platform like CommentSold to broadcast there and accept orders. Nifty!

DAY 2: BOOST ENTERTAINMENT WITH SOFTWARE & APPS

For the most part, you'll get everything you need from your live selling platform. But software and apps can help you boost your live event's entertainment value and manage things behind the scenes in ways that sometimes can't be done on popular live selling platforms alone.

TOP APPS

SWITCHER STUDIO
The ability to use multiple camera angles adds variety and depth to your livestreams and lets you capture every detail of your products. It integrates nicely with multiple platforms like Facebook, YouTube and Shopify.

BEST OF THE REST
Several alternatives to Switcher Studio exist, each with their own strengths and weaknesses.

LIVE CUT

MANYCAM

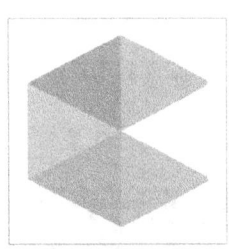

CINAMAKER

SOLDLIVE
Simplifies the process of selling products during live streams on platforms that don't feature live selling like Facebook.

QUICK TIP
Though many of these tools can seamlessly connect to multiple live selling platforms, focus first on just a few to better connect with your true audience.

SIMPLICITYDX
Turn your content into engaging micro-sites that are personalized and easy to shop.

CANVA
Not a graphic designer? No problem. You can create professional-looking graphics for countdown timers, video thumbnails, social media posts, marketing materials, the list goes on, using its drag-and-drop interface and already-made-for-you templates. And do it all for free!

BIGVU
Runs through your script right on your screen as you talk. This helps you remember all your talking points while looking directly at the camera, making you look more natural and confident.

SHOPIFY
It's like an all-in-one. Here's why: Create and run your online store easily. It syncs with your social media channels. Smooth checkouts make sales a breeze. And it offers a bunch of marketing, SEO and inventory tools that help you scale and go international.

WOOCOMMERCE
Takes your WordPress site and turns it into a full-fledged online store. It covers everything like product sales, payment processing and inventory management. This makes it a great tool for live sellers because it links your live events with an awesome online presence.

38 | GEARING UP FOR THE JOURNEY

DAY 2: HOW TO
GET & KEEP
YOUR SELLER ACCOUNT

When live selling on any platform, you must stick to their specific policies, which generally includes your eligibility for opening a selling account, the rules you need to follow to continue selling and the ongoing fees you must pay.

GETTING YOUR ACCCOUNT

QUICK TIP
Even if you didn't need followers to open an account on some platforms, having an existing following makes selling live a million times easier.

Eligibility requirements for live selling accounts vary by platform, and can include things like:

- your age
- where you live
- ID to prove who you are
- having a seller account
- official business documents
- a minimum number of followers
- acceptance of T&Cs

You can check the eligibility criteria of your chosen platforms on their website.

KEEPING YOUR ACCOUNT

It's essential you follow the rules of your chosen platforms, so you don't get penalized or banned.
Key points to remember when live selling on any platform:

- **Products**: Be honest about specs and condition.
- **Claims**: No hype, stick to the facts when talking about product features.
- **Legal**: Make sure you and your products comply with local laws, and don't sell fake or illegal stuff.
- **Pricing**: List all costs upfront, prices, shipping, taxes, the whole shebang.
- **Returns**: Make returns simple and clear, no one likes a confusing process.
- **Content**: Play by the platform's rules. Language, images and behavior should all be on point.

PAYING FOR YOUR ACCOUNT

A lot of platforms have the same costs, with many only charging you when you make a sale.
Some common fees and when you'll face them:

- **Listing Fee**: Cost to list your products on the platform. Free on most platforms.
- **Transaction Fee**: Charged every time you make a sale. The rate can vary by product category.
- **Payment Processing Fee**: Charged for payment processing services, like Stripe or credit cards.
- **Fulfilment Fee**: Shipping costs based on product category, weight and size.
- **Cost of Goods**: What you spend on your products.
- **Storage Fee**: Monthly charges based on the space your inventory needs.
- **Returns**: Costs for handling returns and restocking.
- **Marketing**: Expenses for promoting your products.
- **Tax**: Various taxes depending on your location.

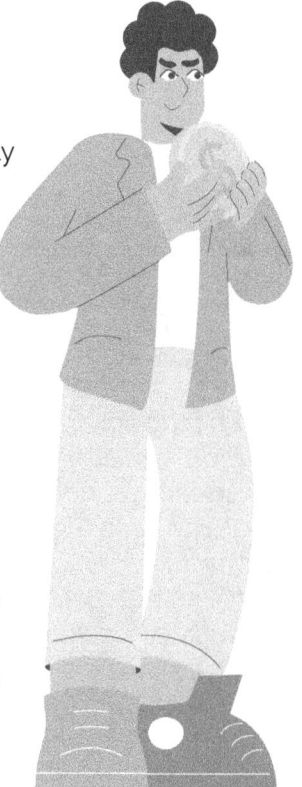

Once you work out true cost of running your business, you'll know how to price your products.

DAY 2: CREATING & OPTIMIZING
YOUR SELLER ACCOUNT

To create a seller account (or "business" account), number one it's completely free and number two you don't even need to be a registered business. Now that might depend on where you live, so please check with the rules on your chosen platform in your country.

PRO HACK

Tools like Flodesk and Taplink let you add multiple links in your bio. You simply create a landing page and place all your links on it, sending viewers to where you want them to go.

1 Navigate to your chosen platform and hit the link to register as a seller. If you already have a personal account there, you might need to log in to that first and then apply for a seller account. Check that you're eligible for a seller account (see the previous page for details).

2 Enter all your business and contact info, being extra sure you've selected the right region as that could cause issues with shipping, tax and so on. Don't decide on a username (or shop name) and profile pic at this point in time. If you absolutely have to select a username and upload a profile pic as part of the sign-up process, skip to Day 5 for tips on how to craft your brand identity, and then come back here to continue setting up your account.

LEARNING BEST PRACTICES

Many platforms offer learning hubs, teaching you everything you need to know to get started on their ecosystems and learning tips and tricks to succeed. There's TikTok Shop Academy, Amazon Seller University and Shopify Academy to name just three.

Don't worry too much about trying to go through every tutorial and watch every how-to video. Think of the learning hubs as a place to refine your approach, get answers when you need them and discover updates on policies and features.

Enter your bank information. Not because they'll take money from you, but so they can pay you your revenue or royalties from sales. You'll also be asked to provide your tax information like your Social Security Number, National Insurance number, or similar. You'll probably be asked to fill out form W-9 if you're a US worker that has an SSN or TIN, or a W-8 form if you're a non-US resident who gets income from US sources.

Submit your ID documents for verification. This is a vital step for your platform's compliance, so can't be skipped. You usually need to upload your passport or driver's license. While the admins are checking your docs, you should be able to optimize your account, but not yet post product listings. Add a link to your website and connect all your social channels. You can now start thinking about your shop name and other brand elements.

DAY 3: CHOOSING A
PROFITABLE NICHE

To succeed in live selling, you need to carve out a niche. Choosing the right one means selecting the best target market for your products. When starting out, aim to become the go-to seller in your niche. This approach helps build trust with potential buyers and boosts your sales.

When you're picking a niche for selling on social media, think about what you love, your skills and what your audience wants. Check out existing niches and competitors. For example, if you love yoga and know a lot about it, sell yoga gear and offer tips.

LIVE SHOPPING TOP-SELLING CATEGORIES

#1 Clothing

Skin care

Accessories

Body care

Luxury goods

Electronics

Furniture & Decor

Consumables

NICHE DOWN, MAKE MORE MONEY

Niching down means focusing on a smaller market segment, which can be smarter than going mainstream. It's less competitive, easier to market to and reaches an underserved audience. You'll also have a better chance of winning customers by speaking directly to their needs. That means you still get big sales but with less marketing effort.

CLOTHING
Virtual try-before-you-buy experiences are in. Zero in on a specific segment to meet unique customer needs. Some of the biggest sellers are vintage wear, activewear and one-of-a-kind styles. Just be ready to put in extra effort to attract loyal buyers.

SKIN CARE
Seeing real-time results makes skin care products super appealing. You could focus on vegan or organic options. Sourcing these products might cost more, but you'll be selling safer, eco-friendly choices.

ACCESSORIES
Showcasing the style and functionality of worn or carried accessories, like hats, bags, eyewear and artisanal jewelry instantly makes them a hit. Sharing your story and what makes your products special can help you stand out.

BODY CARE
Customers trust body care products more when they can see benefits firsthand. Good research and high standards will build trust and loyalty among your audience.

LUXURY GOODS
Highlighting exclusivity in live interactions makes luxury goods shine. Many luxury brands prefer in-house marketing or only partner with top influencers.

ELECTRONICS
Electronics really come to life when showing off their features and how they work in real-time. Keeping up with the latest trends means your products will always be fresh and exciting for your audience.

FURNITURE & DECOR
A virtual showroom experience can draw in decor enthusiasts. Creating minimalist designs or custom pieces attracts customers who love unique looks. Sourcing materials and keeping up quality can be tricky, but your niche audience will appreciate it.

CONSUMABLES
Taste tests and demos make selling consumables fun. Offering specialty snacks or craft beverages caters to food lovers. Standing out with unique flavors or health benefits helps attract dedicated customers.

DAY 3: IDENTIFYING YOUR TARGET AUDIENCE

If you're trying to reach everyone, you'll reach no one. You'll get viewers watching you, and some looking at your products, but your live events won't appeal to any specific group of people if you don't have a specific viewer in mind. That's why it's essential to find your target audience.

WHO ARE YOUR IDEAL VIEWERS?

Your target audience is like a subcategory of people who are interested in products in your niche. Like if you sell in the men's gym wear niche, your ideal viewers could be hardcore gym buffs who demand function and durability in their gym wear, fashion-forward fitness enthusiasts in their twenties looking for stylish activewear, or older, budget-conscious beginners wanting something affordable to kick-start their fitness journey. Or it could be all three. It's good to have more than one target audience within your target niche, with three being the most common.

When you've narrowed down who these people you want to target are, it makes your life easier because then you can focus your efforts with them in mind:

- **Live events**: Tailor your script, product demos and interactions to their interests, making engagement more meaningful.
- **Marketing**: Craft content that captures their attention and speaks directly to their needs, increasing conversions and brand loyalty.
- **Research**: Collect insights from analytics and direct competitors to help you improve your product selection, pricing and viewer experiences.

It's not an exact science. And knowing your ideal viewers doesn't mean that your products and pricing will always hit the mark and that every live event will be a guaranteed success. You also might not know yet who'll engage with you and buy your stuff.

The best place to start is by looking at your existing followers. From there, you can look at your social and, if you have one, your website analytics. Finally, take notes on your competition; their brand, their messaging and who they're targeting. Here's an example of how to define a target audience for the men's gym wear niche.

EXAMPLE AUDIENCE: MEN'S FITNESS

DEMOGRAPHICS

Age range: 18-25
Gender: 90% M, 10% F
Ethnicity: 60% White, 40% Black
Location: Urban areas on the East Coast, USA
Income level: $35-55,000
Job: Entry-level, Student

PSYCHOGRAPHICS

Interests: Running, lifting weights, sports, Crossfit
Values: Physical and mental health, healthy eating

ROLE MODELS

Simeon Panda, Steve Cook, Mat Fraser, Cristiano Ronaldo

CHALLENGES

- Feeling pressured by gym culture and social media to wear high-end, status-driven fitness apparel
- Lack of variety for fitness gear that's practical yet affordable
- Finding gear that looks good on the way to the gym not just at the gym

GETS INFO FROM

- Facebook (following athletes and influencers)
- YouTube (sporting events and product demos)
- Search engines (reviews and comparisons)

When you've filled in the details like I have in the example above, you'll have a detailed description of someone who represents your ideal viewer.

GEARING UP FOR THE JOURNEY

DAY 3: SOURCING YOUR
PRODUCTS

One of the most important (and overwhelming) first steps in live selling is figuring out what to sell and how to get those products into your viewers' hands. Without the right product selection, suppliers and fulfillment strategy, I'm afraid it won't matter how entertaining or engaging you are, your efforts will fall flat.

Earlier today, you thought about what niche you'd like to sell products in and feel comfortable talking about with your viewers. You also identified your target audience. Now, you need to know where to source your products.

"HOLDING STOCK" FULFILLMENT MODEL

Here are some sourcing options if you choose to buy and store products yourself (at home or in a warehouse) and ship products directly to viewers:

- **Domestic wholesalers** offer fast shipping and easier returns, but they can be pricier. Some better-known US-based wholesalers include Faire (expanding globally), Wholesale Central and Tundra.

- **Direct from manufacturers** means cutting out the middleman, giving you higher margins. But getting direct access to manufacturers can be tough as a small business. You can find manufacturers through online directories and trade shows.

- **Trusted platforms** like eBay and Alibaba give you access to an insane variety of international products at competitive prices, often with low minimum order quantities, making it easier to test new products. Keep in mind that it can come with longer lead times, higher shipping costs and more complex returns.

- **Local artisans and makers** are a great choice because they have unique inventory that are hard for your viewers to find locally. Partner with local creators for handmade or exclusive pieces.

> **PRO HACK**
> Think branding early. Even if you're sourcing generic products now, start branding. This can be anything from custom packaging, stickers with your logo, hand-written Thank You cards, you name it. It really does build customer loyalty and makes your live selling business feel more premium.

"NOT HOLDING STOCK" FULFILLMENT MODEL

Here are some sourcing options if you choose to take orders from your viewers but have them handled and shipped by the supplier or manufacturer:

- **Dropshipping** is a low-risk business model because you don't keep any stock on hand. But altho it's less expensive to start, profit margins are usually lower. You also have less control over things like product quality and supply chain issues.

  There are many websites offering dropshipping. Some of the most popular options include AliExpress, Spocket, AliDropship, DSers, SaleHoo, Modalyst and Zendrop, each with unique features and integrations.

- Minimum order quantities (MOQs) from wholesalers can be an expensive mistake. That's why many people start out with **affiliate products**, like the affiliate feature on TikTok Shop, letting you test products *before* holding inventory.

TIPS FOR SOURCING PRODUCTS

- Aim to have a preferred supplier for a product and at least one backup. This helps if viewers find a product out of stock.
- Make sure the products you source comply with local laws and regulations; another reason to choose domestic suppliers.

- If you hold stock, always test products in small batches (or get samples, if you can and if applicable). So, instead of committing to 500 units, start with 20–50. See what sells fast on your live events and reorder only your top performers.

Your early days will be full of trial and error. That's a good thing! Learn from your viewers, gather feedback and use it to improve your product lineup.

DAY 3: BUILD RELATIONSHIPS WITH
SUPPLIERS & VENDORS

Building great relationships with who you get your products from makes selling so much easier! As a live seller, you need dependable inventory and consistent pricing. When you build trust with your suppliers, you not only get access to better pricing and higher-quality products, but you also reduce problems like stock shortages and shipping delays, making your sales run more smoothly and keeping your viewers happy.

I've seen it first-hand with a vendor I once worked with. A viewer needed a last-minute dress for a wedding and needed it like yesterday. She liked the one I was selling but my shipping times would've meant it arrived after the ceremony. Because I had a great connection with my vendor, they agreed to put her order at the front of the queue and ship it out same day.

SET CLEAR EXPECTATIONS

Setting expectations early prevents future disagreements and complications. By spelling out what you're both responsible for from the start, there's less room for misunderstandings, and trust between you can develop naturally over time.

Of course, this isn't something you just chat about. It's set out in an agreement because you need to be confident that suppliers deliver quality products without defects, just as your suppliers need assurance that you'll pay them fairly and on time.

MAINTAIN OPEN, CONSISTENT COMMUNICATION

Depending on your sales model, you might never speak to a human being in real-time. Just be aware of communication channels that are open to you in case you need them in an emergency. And if you do have regular check-ins, ask questions and be transparent about concerns. That way you can work through challenges together.

MONITOR POTENTIAL RISKS

Risk is a natural part of any business, but planning ahead minimizes those risks. The best way to do that involves three actions: 1. pinpoint risks in your partnership, 2. develop strategies to manage them and 3. keep reassessing potential risks and adjusting your strategies together as needed.

WORK WITH MORE THAN ONE SUPPLIER

One of your biggest risks is relying on a single supplier. This is especially true in current unpredictable markets where things like the tariffs imposed on goods imported to the US by President Trump can make it harder and more expensive to source your products from other countries. So, if your only supplier experiences delays or shortages, your entire operation is affected. Having relationships with multiple vendors gives you more control over pricing, product availability and keeps your business going.

OTHER OPPORTUNITIES

Strong relationships with your suppliers can open doors you didn't expect. Take time to understand the goals and challenges of your vendors and then discuss ways you can help each other.

DAY 3: HOW TO NEGOTIATE PRICES & TERMS

Negotiating payment prices and terms is essentially setting the prices, timeframe and process for paying your suppliers. This conversation usually starts at the time you place your order.

Better payment terms allow you to keep cash longer, improving your ability to pay bills and reducing your exposure to risks like if your supplier faces financial challenges.

QUICK TIP

If you plan on using dropshipping or if your prices are fixed right now, this advice might not fit your current setup. That's okay; return when your approach shifts. You'll find it useful then.

ONE SUPPLIER AT A TIME

If you sell products that need to be specially created for you in a supply chain, then you'll really only deal with one supplier. But if you do have more than one, then prioritize them and deal with the supplier you spend the most money with first. It helps if they're a large company because they're in a better position to agree to bigger discounts for bulk orders and longer payment periods.

KNOW YOUR STUFF BEFORE YOU BEGIN

Before you pick up the phone or write an email, it's wise to gather some facts. Look up average prices for the items you need and look at what others in your niche pay. This is the time to learn about your product's market and cost standards. With this data, you can set a target range for your deal. Good talks start with good facts.

BOND FOR BETTER TRADE

As you learned on previous pages, every chance to speak to your supplier is a chance to build a bond. So, stay friendly and listen well. Ask clear questions, such as "Can we talk about the price?" or "What is included in this term?" These open words create a space where both you and your supplier feel at ease. You'll get a better result by being honest and friendly rather than simply threatening to use an alternative, cheaper supplier.

SET YOUR GOALS AND KNOW YOUR LIMITS

Before the chat starts, set your goals. You should think about what you need most. Is it a lower price, quicker delivery, better payment terms, or the chance to order in bulk? You may also decide on the lowest price you're willing to pay, or what's the best payment period.

BE OPEN TO A GIVE AND TAKE

At the same time, know where you can give a bit. Maybe you can live with product prices if you pay for them much later, or you can order a larger quantity to drop the cost. Remember, your aim is not to win at all cost but to create a deal where both sides feel good. When both feel safe to give a little, a long-lasting trade can begin, so be prepared to compromise. You might suggest moving your standard 30-day payment window to 120 days but in the end settle for paying half after 45 days and the other half after 90 days.

WRITING YOUR GOALS AS A LIST HELPS

This list acts as a map for the chat. It shows where you must stay firm and where you can bend a bit. When you speak with your supplier, use your list for reference. This way, you do not stray far from what you need.

GEARING UP FOR THE JOURNEY
DAY 3: A WORD ABOUT
LUXURY BRANDS

High-end brands are all about exclusivity, top-notch quality and amazing customer experiences. Established brands have high production costs and typically work with well-known influencers, celebrities, in-house experts or even the designers themselves to maintain their premium positioning and credibility as a luxury brand.

Here's a prime example: the Spanish fashion brand Zara debuted their new livestream concept on Douyin in China in 2023. It was a carefully choreographed setup with 12 cameras, 50 professionals, a 9,000-square-meter set and hosted by supermodel You Tianyi.

That being said, some luxury brands have shifted from glossy, music-video-style streams to authentic at-home tutorials, live Q&As, poetry readings and intimate live performances. And social media users love the genuine vibes from designers like Mulberry and Chanel. Brandon Maxwell, for instance, regularly checks in with his followers on Instagram Live, sharing thoughts, feelings and advice, while encouraging questions. Marc Jacobs also hosts informal streams with fans.

This casual content works for them, but again it's the designers and brands who control what gets broadcast to ensure it aligns with their image.

So, does that mean the luxury segment is totally out of reach for live sellers starting out?

A DISTANT GOAL WORTH STRIVING FOR?

Here are some things you'll be up against as a new live seller. They're just to show you why it's tough (but not impossible) to break into the luxury segment:

- **HIGH PRODUCTION COSTS**: Creating high-quality, professional livestreams that look expensive is expensive. Starting out, it's near impossible to afford the production quality that luxury brands demand, and I don't recommend splashing out at this stage.

- **BRAND RECOGNITION AND CREDIBILITY**: Established luxury brands have strong recognition and credibility. Building brand credibility takes time and a rather substantial investment in marketing and partnerships.

- **ACCESS TO INFLUENCERS AND CELEBRITIES**: Well-known brands exclusively collaborate with high-profile influencers and celebrities. If you're not already well-known, you need to focus on building your brand before high-profile brands will want to partner with you.

- **MAINTAINING EXCLUSIVITY**: Luxury brands thrive on exclusivity. Creating a sense of exclusivity just won't be possible for new sellers as it requires careful curation and a well-defined brand identity, which again takes time to develop.

For live sellers starting out like you, I'd say it's more practical to focus on getting better at hosting, improving your product quality and gradually increasing your reach before diving into the luxury livestream space.

But when you're ready and you have the resources and audience, for sure dive right in because the opportunities are vast for anyone breaking into this exclusive market.

DAY 4: ORDER PROCESSING & FULFILLMENT SYSTEM

Live shopping events generate lots of activity. This means high sales volumes in a very short period. That's why you need a well-organized order processing system to help you handle orders efficiently from the moment a viewer makes a purchase to the final delivery.

For your customers, a seamless fulfillment process gives them a good experience, leading to repeat business and positive reviews. For you, it means less chance of making mistakes and saves you time from getting too involved in the process.

You'll learn more about how to further streamline and automate your order process later on in this book. For now, though, put your order processing system together using these key components:

Order Placement

Simplify the order placement process for your viewers. Give clear instructions for placing orders, including shipping options and all the payment methods you accept. For example, use a clean and intuitive checkout page with minimal steps, offering multiple payment options like credit cards, PayPal and mobile wallets.

Order Confirmation

Let your viewers know right away that their order went through. Send an email with order details and delivery times. Give them tracking info so they can see where their package is. Use their name and thank them for buying. For example, after a purchase, send an email with the subject "Thanks for Your Order, [Customer Name]! Your Order #[Order Number] is Confirmed."

Inventory Management

Keep track of your stock to avoid running out if a bunch of orders come in at once. Use an inventory system that updates as orders come in and set alerts for low stock to restock quickly. For example, use a system like WooCommerce or Shopify for real-time tracking and automated alerts.

Order Fulfillment

If using a *reliable* dropshipping company, they'll handle picking, packing and shipping, printing labels and sending tracking updates to you and your viewers. If shipping products yourself, organize your space for easy picking and packing. Always work with a trustworthy shipping carrier even if it means spending more on postage as there's nothing worse than chasing up late and lost packages.

Customer Comms

Keep customers informed throughout the order processing journey. Send regular updates on their order status, including shipping and delivery notifications like "Your Order Has Shipped!" and "Your Order Is Out for Delivery." Automate these messages if you can and you'll save a ton of time.

Returns and Refunds

It's a sad reality but returns happen in any business. Make your return and refund process hassle-free for customers. You could provide prepaid return labels and simple instructions for returning items. And process refunds quickly to keep customer trust and satisfaction.

> Test your ordering process from start to finish. Place an order, see how delivery goes and then try returning the item. Note any hiccups and aim to fix them for a smoother experience.

DAY 4: CALCULATING YOUR COSTS

Calculating costs and margins allows you to set competitive prices, manage expenses and create irresistible deals. You'll read more about pricing and deals on the next pages. For now, though, let's talk costs.

Your goal here is to identify all the costs associated with your products and operations. Typically, you'll need to factor in the following:

- **Cost of Goods Sold (COGS)**: The direct costs of producing your products, including materials, labor and manufacturing. For example, if you sell handmade jewelry, your COGS includes materials like beads, wire and clasps, as well as the time spent crafting each piece.
- **Overhead Costs**: Indirect costs such as storage, salaries, software and tools, platform fees, tax and marketing expenses.
- **Order Fulfillment**: Costs associated with packaging and shipping products to customers.
- **Returns**: Depends on the return rate. At first you can estimate this. Charging customers for return shipping and/or a restocking fee can help offset your expenses when processing returns; but these policies can hurt customer satisfaction as many consumers expect free returns.

I've given examples on the next page breaking down the costs of selling three different products and what you can expect to make in profit when you sell each item.

It's important to list your costs in this way, being as precise as you can for each. I'll explain why using the examples across the page:

DRESS
A "healthy" profit margin generally falls between 10% and 20% of your product price, with 10% considered a good baseline. You're making just 5.2% with this dress. Make a better deal with your supplier or switch.

BAG
A typical range for advertising spend as a percentage of product price is between 5% and 20%. As a new seller, you'll probably spend more at first. But at 22%, marketing costs are really eating into profits.

BOOK
Costs are super low because each book is printed on demand. But the profit margin is a very low 15%, making it not worth the time you're putting in. Lower ad costs and a higher retail price can help.

THE TRUE COST OF SELLING ONLINE

	 Dress retail price $59	 Bag retail price $140	 Book retail price $18
COST OF GOODS SOLD	$25.68	$38.95	$3.77
ORDER FULFILLMENT	$3.95	$7.90	$2.95
STORAGE (OPTIONAL)	$1.62	$0.50	$0
PRODUCT RETURNS	$2.75	$4.48	$0
ADVERTISING	$5.00	$31.40	$2.82
STAFF AND SOFTWARE	$3.50	$1.96	$0.52
PLATFORM FEES	$3.58	$4.58	$1.57
INCOME TAX	$9.80	$32.00	$3.60
	Profit **$3.12**	Profit **$18.23**	Profit **$2.77**

WHAT YOU'LL GET WHEN YOU SELL EACH ITEM

*Guide prices only. Figures vary depending on where you live and your business model.

QUICK TIP

The income you make from live selling is taxable. Don't forget to factor in those pesky taxes when you're calculating your costs and margins. **BUT** be sure to claim your business expenses like equipment, software and subscriptions to lighten your tax load.

… | GEARING UP FOR THE JOURNEY

DAY 4: COMPETITIVE PRICING
FOR PROFIT

Now that you know your costs, or at least you've got a rough idea of costs, you can start thinking about how much you'll sell each product for. Too high, and people might not buy; too low, and you might not cover your costs.

But pricing isn't just about covering costs. You have to think about how much a product is worth to your viewers. When it comes to shopping, people often decide what to buy based on how good and valuable they think something is. Higher prices usually make people think the product is better, while lower prices can make them see it as not-so-great. This link between price and quality is super important, especially when there's a lot of competition.

And that brings me to a very important part in the process of setting competitive prices: Your competitors.

Start by identifying who your main competitors are in the market. These are people or businesses that sell similar products to the same target audience as well as people or businesses that offer different products that meet the same customer needs as yours.

Gather detailed pricing data from your competitors' websites, ecommerce platforms and other relevant sources like social media stores. Use price comparison tools like Google Shopping and PriceGrabber to quickly gather and compare competitor prices. Log everything in a spreadsheet.

Now use the collected data to benchmark your prices against competitors. Ensure your prices are competitive without compromising profitability.

But if you are setting higher prices, make sure you can justify your pricing with unique features, quality or benefits. Another advantage of setting higher prices is that it gives you the chance to lower the price while still making money. You'll learn more about discounts and deals on the next page.

This is also a good time to spot any gaps in the market where you can position your products effectively, as well as looking at how your competitors price different product tiers or bundles.

TL;DR PRICING FOR PROFIT PROCESS

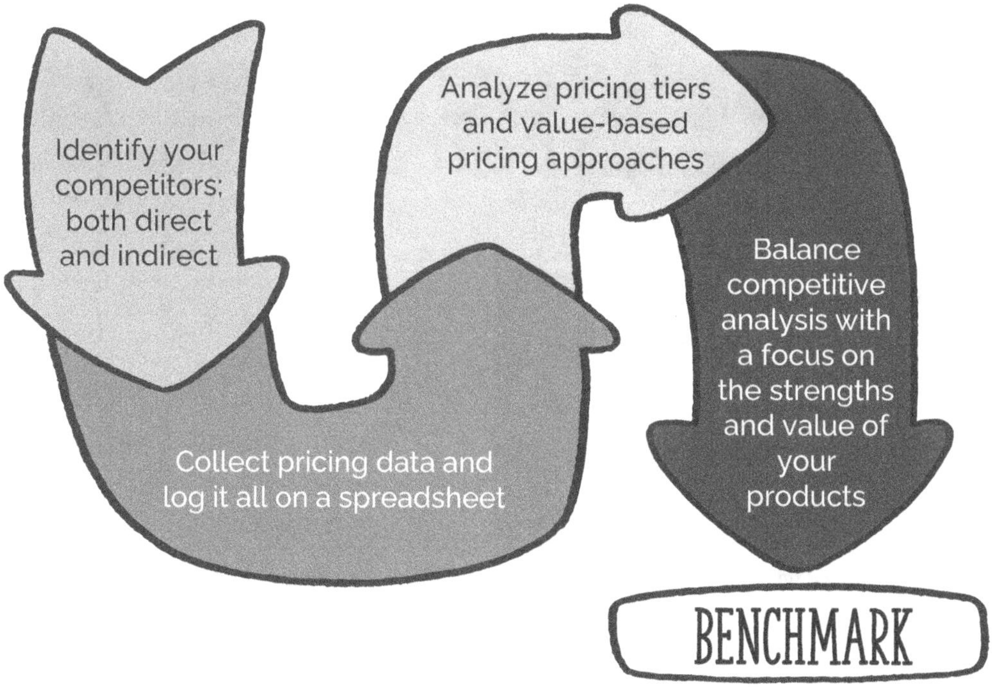

- Identify your competitors; both direct and indirect
- Analyze pricing tiers and value-based pricing approaches
- Collect pricing data and log it all on a spreadsheet
- Balance competitive analysis with a focus on the strengths and value of your products

BENCHMARK

LILY'S HANDMADE SOAPS

Imagine Lily, a creator of handmade soaps who sells them on her website and livestreams.

Lily identified her main competitors as other handmade soap brands and larger natural skincare companies.

She gathered pricing data from competitors' websites, online stores and social media pages.

Lily analyzed competitors' pricing tiers, discounts and value-based pricing approaches.

She benchmarked her prices against competitors and identified areas where she could differentiate her products based on quality and unique ingredients.

She made sure her prices covered her costs and left her with a nice profit, making her efforts worthwhile.

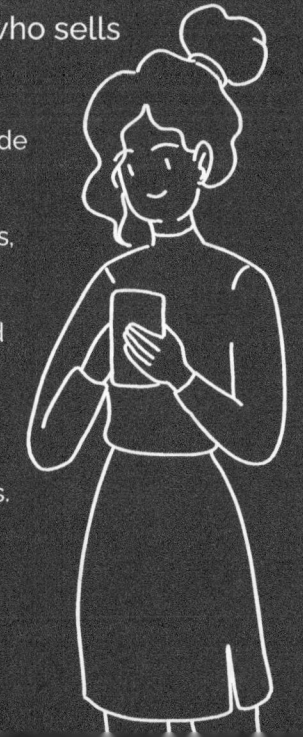

DAY 4: CRAFTING
IRRESISTIBLE DEALS

Creating irresistible deals that resonate with your viewers is an art. Craft good offers and you'll drive long-term success in your live selling business.

Whatever kind of deals you put into action, make sure they're easy to understand, still reflect the quality of your products, align with your audience's interests, and spark excitement. Anything that confuses buyers or hurts the perceived value of your products reduces the appeal of your deal.

OFFERS THAT CAPTIVATE AND CONVERT

#1 Bundle Offers

- **Cross-Selling**: Bundle related products to encourage viewers to buy more.
- **Tiered Bundles**: Offer different tiers of bundles to cater to various customer budgets.
- **Seasonal Bundles**: Create bundles tailored to specific seasons or holidays.

#2 Free Gifts & Add-Ons

- **Low-Cost Gifts**: Include small, low-cost items that add value without significantly impacting your profit margins.
- **Exclusive Add-Ons**: Offer exclusive add-ons that are not available for purchase separately, like a reusable shopping bag.
- **Limited-Time Gifts**: Rotate free gifts to keep the offers fresh and exciting.

#3 Loyalty Programs

- **Points System**: Viewers earn points for every purchase and can redeem them for discounts or free products.
- **Tiered Rewards**: Create tiers with increasing rewards based on viewer-spending levels.
- **Exclusive Perks**: Like early access to sales, special discounts or VIP events for regular viewers.

#4 Buy More, Save More

- **Volume Discounts**: Provide discounts that increase with the quantity purchased.
- **Spend Thresholds**: Offer discounts or free shipping for orders that exceed a certain value.
- **Tiered Pricing**: Create tiered pricing that rewards viewers for buying more.

#5 Referral Programs

- **Referral Discounts**: Reward viewers for referring friends and family with discounts or store credits to both the referrer and the referred customer.
- **Bonus Rewards**: Offer additional rewards for viewers who refer multiple people.

#6 Personalized Offers

- **Targeted Discounts**: Send personalized discount codes to viewers based on their purchase history and preferences.
- **Birthday Offers**: Offer special deals or discounts for viewers on their birthday.
- **Anniversary Rewards**: Celebrate viewer anniversaries with exclusive offers or gifts.

62 | GEARING UP FOR THE JOURNEY

DAY 5: YOUR USP:

WHAT SETS YOU APART?

At its core, your Unique Selling Proposition (USP) explains why your live selling events and products are different and/or better than other sellers who are competing for attention from the same audience. It's your vibe, your story, your special approach. Summed up simply and concisely:

What do you offer that no-one else does in your market?

CRAFTING AN AWESOME USP

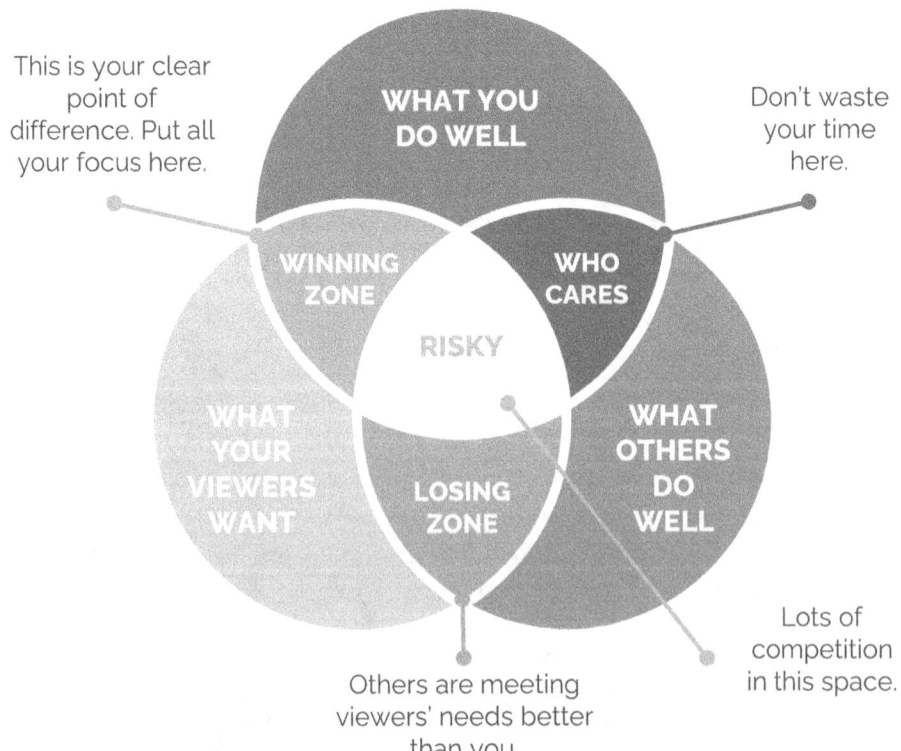

WHAT YOU DO WELL

List what makes you or your products unique. Be specific. For example, saying "My products are high-quality" is too generic and your competitors can easily say the same thing. Instead, think how you or your product addresses gaps that others miss.

WHAT OTHERS DO WELL

Research your competition and list their USPs. Your goal isn't to compete with them, but rather to find gaps where you can carve out your own unique space where you're the go-to choice for your viewers.

WHAT YOUR VIEWERS WANT

Low price, high quality and fast delivery are too generic. You need to look deeper to understand what your viewers would pay more for or wait longer for because it meets their specific needs and challenges.

USP EXAMPLE FOR INSPIRATION

Tattly creates temporary tattoos using sophisticated artwork.

Their USP: **Fake tattoos by real artists**

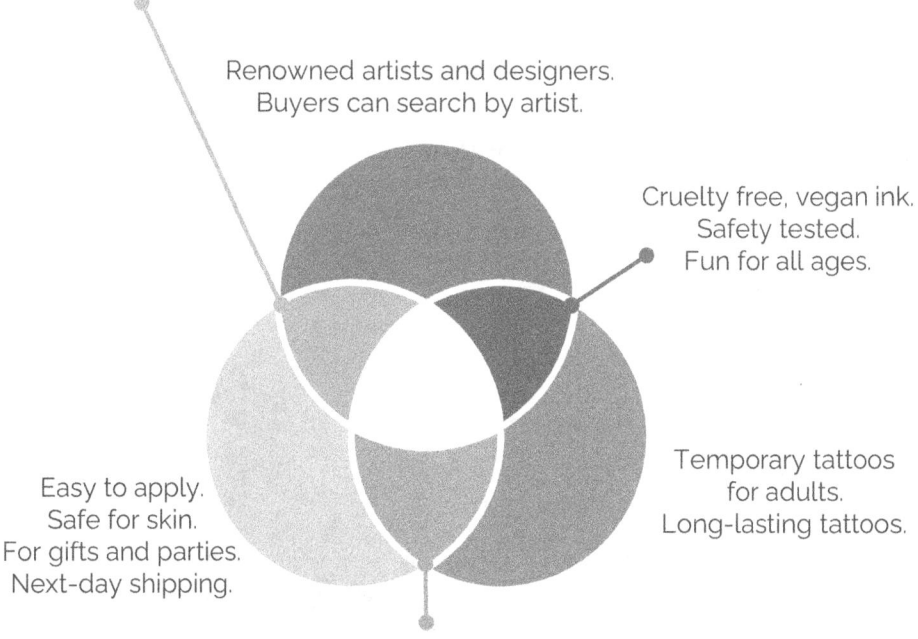

Renowned artists and designers. Buyers can search by artist.

Cruelty free, vegan ink. Safety tested. Fun for all ages.

Easy to apply. Safe for skin. For gifts and parties. Next-day shipping.

Temporary tattoos for adults. Long-lasting tattoos.

Bulk order discounts. Custom printed tattoos.

DAY 5: CRAFTING YOUR BRAND
IDENTITY

Top streamers stand out because their branding is consistent and memorable. Their name, logo, design, style, content, and so on are instantly recognizable to their followers.

To help you stand out and make a name for yourself in the live selling world, you'll need to follow in their footsteps as you start building your own visual identity.

The good news is your brand and your streams can be customized with any look and feel you want. The only downside to that is if you want to make a big branding change in the future after it's already become established. For that reason, it's important to have good branding in place before your first live stream. You don't need everything to be 100% perfect from the jump, but you'll want to at least have the basics.

Let's start with **NAME**
Picking the right username can be tricky, but it's worth getting right. Go for something catchy and easy to remember that fits your brand values, or the products you sell if you sell things in a certain niche exclusively.

Your viewers will likely call you by your username, so keep that in mind too. For example, a live seller of plant products might pick "FernElla" instead of "PlantLover123" because viewers can still refer to you as Ella. It's also way more personal and fitting with the brand vibe.

Start by brainstorming lots of name ideas. Use tools like name generators, word lists and thesauruses. Jot down everything, even the silly ones! Once you've got a list of names, narrow it down by cutting ones that are too long, too generic, too hard to spell, or too similar to other streamers.

Before settling on a name, test it out. Say it aloud or try it on a logo or banner. You can also ask a supportive friend what they think.

Once you've chosen a name, and you feel happy and confident using it, register it as a domain and secure social media handles to protect it and keep others from using it.

On some platforms, usernames can only be changed after a certain number of days, and on others not at all, so choose thoughtfully (and I hope the one you want isn't already taken by someone else!).

COLORS
A handful of colors (3 to 5) is all you need to make your brand feel connected and stand out. Using colors that match your message, like green for eco-friendly and blue for trust, gives viewers the impression you want. Tools like Coolors can help you pick shades that work well together without overloading your palette.

LOGO
Now that you've nailed down your username and colors, creating a logo is the next step. Stick to something simple, like your initials, or choose an icon that really speaks to what your brand is about and then add your brand colors. If you need help, there are a bunch of tools out there that can create a logo in seconds. I use Canva a lot, and I highly recommend it.
Bonus tip: a great logo works beautifully on merch!

PROFILE IMAGE
A photo of yourself works great as a profile picture. If you're on multiple platforms, use the same image across all social accounts. You can also use your logo if that feels right.

DAY 5: DESIGNING YOUR BRAND'S
VISUAL (& AUDIO) ELEMENTS

Cohesive, consistent and strong visuals make a big difference, as they set you apart and help you stand out from the crowd of other streamers.

VISUAL BRANDING ESSENTIALS

QUICK TIP

Building your brand takes time, and it'll grow and change along the way. At some point in the future, you'll start looking to have professionally designed branding. Your goal at the outset, however, is to have consistent visuals that are a step above a generic template and plain text.

Ready-Made Templates
SAVES TIME AND KEEPS LAYOUTS CONSISTENT

I recommend spending time teaching yourself how to create basic yet strong visuals. It'll be a valuable skill in the long run and even learning just a wee bit can do wonders.

That doesn't mean starting from scratch though. You can find cool templates on Canva or Adobe Express (both free to use and intuitive) and tweak them to match your branding.

Design tools let you easily resize graphics to suit different purposes, but many keep this feature behind a paywall. You can still do it on the free account, but it requires more manual steps.

Fonts and Typography
THE RIGHT FONTS SAY A LOT ABOUT YOUR BRAND

You know what it's like trying to read words on a YouTube thumbnail on your phone. That's why simple, easy-to-read fonts work best.

Let your font reflect your branding. For example, a playful font for a fun brand or a sleek design for something more professional.

Too many fonts can distract from your message, so aim for one or two at most. Here are some ideas pairing a bold header with simple body text to create a well-balanced look.

Your Signature Style
A UNIFIED LOOK MAKES A LASTING IMPRESSION

Potential elements you'll need visuals for can include:

- Thumbnails
- Overlays
- Banners
- Profiles
- Pre-show countdowns
- Backgrounds
- Product images
- Website

Define one editing style, typography and color palette for your visuals and stick with it. As with anything, consistency builds trust and makes your brand memorable.

> Some platforms let you configure audio alerts, meaning a short snippet of sound is played whenever an event occurs like at the end of a countdown or when a viewer completes a purchase. Viewers can find them cute or annoying. But if you use them, the same rules on branding and consistency apply.

YOU TOTALLY GOT THIS

Turn what you've learned into progress!

DAY 1:

- ❏ Prepare a dedicated, distraction-free space.
- ❏ Gather essential equipment.
- ❏ Test and fine-tune your lighting angles.

DAY 2:

- ❏ Pick streaming software that fits your needs.
- ❏ Choose a platform to host your live sessions.
- ❏ Register for your seller account.

DAY 3:

- ❏ Choose a niche and identify your target audience.
- ❏ Source products and choose a selling model.
- ❏ Connect and build relationships with suppliers.

DAY 4:

❑ Calculate costs of running your business.

❑ Set pricing to maximize profits.

❑ Explore promos that benefit you and viewers.

DAY 5:

❑ Define your unique selling proposition (USP).

❑ Craft a consistent look and feel for your brand.

❑ Create eye-catching, branded graphics.

PREPPING FOR THE SPOTLIGHT

DAY 6: DESIGN YOUR
SHOW'S DNA

This is your big-picture strategy. Think of it as laying down the foundation or blueprint for your live selling event. Here's what you need to think about when structuring your show format.

SEGMENT PLANNING

A well-structured show keeps your viewers engaged and stops you feeling disorganized. You'll introduce yourself of course, but then you want to structure the rest of your event for sales through storytelling. Include segments for product demos, interacting with viewers, social proof and letting viewers know how to buy your products. Be thoughtful about how you group segments together in a way that keeps the flow going. In your closing, wrap up your event with a recap of the show, a reminder of how to shop, an invitation for your next event, a teaser about the next event, a thank you for tuning in and send viewers off a great big goodbye!

SHOW DURATION AND FREQUENCY

The ideal length of a live selling event can vary, but a good rule of thumb is to aim for 30 minutes to an hour. This gives you enough time to showcase your products, engage with viewers and answer questions without being too lengthy and overwhelming your audience.

Stick to a consistent schedule so your viewers know when to tune in. Consistency helps build a loyal following. Going live for half an hour on the same day and at the same time every week can be a good starting point. If you want to increase that, add an extra day rather than extend your event. It's easier for your viewers to commit to tuning in for shorter time slots and because keeping events concise lets you to maintain energy, deliver value-packed content and leave viewers wanting more.

GO LIVE & THRIVE - DAY 6 | **73**

AUDIENCE ENGAGEMENT STRATEGY

Engagement is what turns viewers into customers. Some ways to keep them locked into your show include:

- **Storytelling**: Start your show with an interesting story. It doesn't even need to be related to your product. This can be a personal experience, a customer success story or a behind-the-scenes look at your brand.
- **Contests and giveaways**: These are great for creating excitement and boosting engagement. You'll learn more about these on Day 15.
- **Real-time interaction**: Actively engage with your viewers during the show. Respond to comments, answer questions and encourage viewers to participate.

QUICK TIP
Use a mix of strategies to keep your viewers excited and involved. You want to create an interactive environment so that your audience has a reason to stay. See Day 8.

Turn the page to see an example of a visual timeline of a live event with a minute-by-minute breakdown

74 | PREPPING FOR THE SPOTLIGHT
DAY 6: PERFECTING YOUR SHOW
TIMELINE

Break down the timeline of your show into specific time slots, detailing what should happen in each slot. This helps you stay organized and ensures a smooth flow. Here's an **example** of a show rundown lasting 30 minutes:

0-2 MINS

You can never assume everyone who tuned in knows or remembers your name or brand. Also, don't wait for viewers to trickle in. Hit Go LIVE and kick off your live video with energy and purpose by introducing yourself and your brand with a big smile. Keep it engaging but brief, because long-winded intros can cause viewers to lose interest.

Some live sellers like to share the schedule of the event with their viewers because it sets expectations. I don't do it, but it's up to you.

2-5 MINS

Take time to talk about your day and share little details about your life. It helps viewers relate to you, making them more engaged in the experience. It'll feel super weird at first to not focus entirely on selling, but casual chats are key to having lasting relationships with your viewers.

Towards the end of this part, transition into what you want to showcase in this event.

5-15 MINS

You can now naturally flow into a problem you or someone else had and the consequences of not solving it. This lets you talk about the benefits of your product before you start talking about features and it shows your viewers why they need your product before you reveal what it is.

Some viewers might leave at this point, and that's fine. Take it as a sign that they weren't potential buyers, so you don't have to spend time trying to win them over.

15-20 MINS

Now you can connect the dots between each problem and your solution with a product demo.

Make sure your viewers understand why your product is valuable to them. What problem does it solve? How does it improve their lives? If they want specifics, they can ask you live or check your website. Your goal is to help them see why they need it, not just what it does. And always lead with your main benefits.

20-25 MINS

You could talk all day about how great your product is, but it's even more powerful to hear it straight from people who've used it. **Use this time to share customer testimonials.**

You'll learn more about making the most of social proof on Day 19.

25-30 MINS

Invite your audience to ask anything on their minds. If viewers asked questions throughout the live demo, you can answer them now. And if time runs short, don't worry, promise to follow up afterwards.

Wrap up your live event with clear, simple next steps. If your goal is sales, share a direct purchase link, so viewers can take action immediately.

Thank everyone for tuning in and wish them a great day!

30-35 MINS

Make it a regular habit to take a five-minute break to relax and decompress after your live event ends. Let your heart rate slow down and give yourself time to mentally shift gears before starting your post-show activities.

DAY 6: EFFECTIVE PRODUCT DEMOS: UNBOXING

In 2023, there were more than 25 billion views of YouTube videos with "unboxing" in the title. People love watching someone unbox a product because it's like the excitement and anticipation you feel when you get a gift.

Unboxing also reduces return rates. Viewers don't have to second guess what they'll get in the mail. You've already shown them what's in the package. Fewer surprises = fewer returns.

For you, unboxing a product as part of your live event means engaging with your viewers in a real way that's easy for you to prepare. What you'll want to focus on:

- **Storytelling**: Unboxing can be totally unscripted, but you should still think about unfolding the story behind the product's features and design as you guide viewers through the unboxing experience.
- **ASMR – A feast for the senses**: The satisfying rip of tape, the crinkle of plastic, the smooth glide of a box lid, the first touch of a fresh product. Add these little moments to create a rich, immersive experience that sticks with viewers.

DAY 6: EFFECTIVE PRODUCT DEMOS:
IN ACTION

Watching you handle your product in real-time eliminates any doubts your viewers have about buying. The key to a successful demo is knowing what your viewers struggle with and what they want (you should know this already after identifying your target audience on Day 3). Then, you simply shape your demo around the most valuable features that solve their issues.

If you're struggling with targeting a specific audience at this stage, don't worry. Most of the time, viewers just need to see the quality, size and color of your product in real footage, instead of trying to guess it. What you'll want to focus on:

- **Focus on benefits, not features**: Show how your product helps your viewers achieve their goals and solves their problems, using real-world examples where possible. And always lead with your best features/benefits.
- **Show and ~~tell~~ ask**: Zoom in, show your product from multiple angles and demonstrate how it works. Share a user-generated photo or video of a satisfied customer as social proof. Ask viewers to leave a comment if they want to see something again.

DAY 6: HOW TO TALK ABOUT PRODUCTS

Features are the characteristics of your products. It's what they do and what they look like. For a jacket, a feature would be a waterproof outer layer or an adjustable hood.

Advantages are what make those features useful. A waterproof jacket keeps you dry during unexpected rain, and the adjustable hood provides extra protection and comfort in windy conditions.

Benefits are the positive outcomes your viewers experience. With a waterproof jacket, they can enjoy outdoor adventures without worrying about the weather. And it gives them peace of mind, keeping them warm and comfortable, not drenched. I can already picture the commercial, "Stay focused on what you're doing, not on the forecast!"

The **FAB** formula in sales is about pitching Features, Advantages and Benefits. It's a tool salespeople use in product presentations and can be especially powerful during live selling events. This formula helps you connect the dots between what your product has, why it matters and how it helps your viewers personally. Instead of just listing features, FAB lets you tell a story that shows real value, building trust and making your pitch far more persuasive and engaging.

QUICK TIP

Less is more when it comes to product demos. While there's no magic number, research shows that keeping it under 15 minutes for each product is best.

So, you should just talk about your products features, then advantages and then benefits, right? While that would be fine, it's a little more nuanced than that.

HOW TO APPLY THE FAB FORMULA

Viewers will listen to features. They'll enjoy hearing about the advantages. But they buy benefits. Only the outcome, the feeling, the result they're going to get from using your product will make them part with their money. Aim to spend the most time on your product's benefits and lead with the strongest ones.

But it's not a direct F → A → B path, unlike the more advanced AIDA model that you'll learn about on Day 17. Instead, you'll try to weave the Fs, As and Bs into a story to show how each product fits into your viewers' day, solving a problem most people share.

Here's an example:
"I was out walking my dog Angus a couple of weeks ago, and the heavens just opened. I put my hood up, but my face was still getting soaked and I had to squint my eyes just to see two feet in front of me. Has that ever happened to you? Let me know in the comments. Anyways, I went looking for a new jacket. One that'll shield my face too (A), and found this one with an adjustable hood (F). Now I can see where I'm going and I can enjoy being out in the rain as much as he does! (B)"

STORYTELLING MAGIC

You can take some creative liberties with your stories. Exaggeration is fun but ensure the heart of the story stays genuine. Your viewers may not be fact-checking and asking to see receipts, but trust matters!

REPEAT REPEAT REPEAT

Repeating your product's FABs is fine because viewers join your events at different times. Plus, it keeps you talking without coming up with fresh content. Just keep your stories as rough outlines rather than rigid scripts.

DAY 7: OVERCOMING CAMERA SHYNESS

QUICK TIP
You don't have to feel confident on camera to get started. All it takes is the belief that you can learn and your determination to get better boosts your confidence.

Everyone streaming live seems naturally confident on camera, right? Well, not always. My earliest streams. Wow! They were not delivered by someone confident or comfortable on camera. I could chat endlessly with a stranger about topics I know well, no problem. But the moment you put me in front of a camera, I shut down completely.

Know this: Nobody is born knowing how to talk to a camera. It's a skill everyone must learn and develop over time. So, how does someone go from feeling awkward talking to a camera to confidently chatting with loads of viewers?

LIVESTREAMING WITH CONFIDENCE

DO IT AND IT WILL COME

If you're nervous about live streaming, start by recording videos just for yourself, pretending that you're live. Practice and improve until you're comfortable.

The more you do it, the more relaxed you'll feel. After a few practice "live" videos, you might find you're ready for the real thing!

IF YOU LOVE IT, THEY'LL LOVE IT

Viewers can always tell if you're not into your own video, and nothing feels more awkward. Don't get caught up chasing perfection; your studio setup, the background, all the little details. The real magic is in how you connect with the camera. Focus on being yourself, not on being perfect, because that's what truly grows your audience.

WHAT YOU WEAR MATTERS

Have you ever put on an outfit and thought, "This is SO ME!"? It's energizing and gives you the confidence to get out in the world.

The right outfit can make you feel more assured and ready to shine on camera. Choose something comfortable and empowering. When you feel confident, it shows!

JUST BE YOURSELF

The key to engaging and keeping your audience coming back is being your authentic self. You might try acting like a character or being overly bubbly, but that's tough to keep up on camera.

Just be yourself. The YOU that you are in real life. Not everyone will connect with you, but those who do tend to stay loyal.

DO WHAT YOU ENJOY

You don't have to do live selling if it's not for you. It might be popular, but there are plenty of other ways to sell your products online. You don't need to master them all.

Focus on what you enjoy. If you don't find a way to enjoy being live on camera, you're unlikely to stick with live selling, and that's perfectly okay.

YOU'RE SHY? SO WHAT!

Shyness isn't necessarily a bad thing for live streaming. In fact, it can make you seem more relatable and genuine to your viewers. With so many outgoing creators out there, your authenticity can help you stand out. So, don't let shyness hold you back; if you're passionate, it'll shine through. Speak from the heart, and confidence will come with time.

PREPPING FOR THE SPOTLIGHT

DAY 7: DEVELOPING YOUR HOSTING PERSONA

On the previous page, you learned about overcoming camera shyness. And one of the points was to be yourself because pretending to be someone you're not is really hard to maintain. So, it might seem contradictory to turn the page and see a section on developing your hosting persona.

But your persona is not an act. It's not about being louder or waving your arms around like a lunatic. It's about improving your on-camera presence. It's about becoming the most confident, authentic version of yourself. And it's for anyone; whether you're super shy or already as composed as a news anchor during a surprise thunderstorm.

Small tweaks, like practicing or adjusting your delivery, can help you feel more at ease and deliver an engaging live presentation while staying true to who you are.

Here are some tips to help you improve your livestreaming persona:

BE SOMEONE WHO ...

... is comfortable yet energetic

It's tempting, I know, but avoid sitting on your couch when live streaming. Sure, it's the most comfortable seat in the house but it'll sap your energy, and your viewers will pick up on it and tune out. Having a powerful posture (see the next page) while filming, or even standing up, naturally boosts your energy levels because you're projecting a more commanding presence.

... can shoot the breeze

Remember the "lipstick king," Austin Li Jiaqi? Well, he reckons that a crucial factor in successful live selling is the ability to connect with your viewers, sharing personal stories and offering glimpses into your daily life. He said, "The key to unlocking live selling is making sure that you've got a really good person behind the camera or set of people behind the camera who can really engage and build that relationship with your shoppers."

Dedicate plenty of time to talking about your day and letting viewers in on your life. It might be counterintuitive at first to not spend most of a live selling session trying to push products on your viewers, but spending time talking about things that have nothing to do with the products themselves is actually one of the most important parts of the live selling experience and helps build relationships between you and your viewers.

... knows their stuff

From personal experience, your first live sessions will feel like disasters. They won't be btw. But you'll realize just how much you need to talk. Pausing for even a millisecond feels like endless dead air. Sure, you can talk about something unrelated to your product but what if doing so isn't right in that moment? This is especially true in another common experience when you get a tricky question thrown your way and not knowing how to respond.

That's why expertise matters. Every live host needs to know their product inside and out. Having a deep understanding of your products gives you credibility, making your livestream more interesting. When you're an expert, you always have meaningful points to share.

... is on their side

Believing in the product you're selling is crucial, but trust is just as important. Your goal isn't to make money, it's to make money by informing the audience about the product, helping them make a decision to buy or not. You want viewers to be as satisfied with their purchase as you are.

84 | PREPPING FOR THE SPOTLIGHT

DAY 7: SPEAK WITH YOUR
WHOLE SELF

Body language and how you control your voice can help you highlight main points, build a connection, make things interesting and match your message's tone.

Here are four ways to make your live stream more dynamic using body language and voice modulation.

QUICK TIP
In case you don't already, start watching live streams. Tune in regularly to a few of your favorites and notice things they do that appeals to you.

#1 Posture
THE POWER POSE

Your posture sets the tone for your entire presentation. Sitting straight with shoulders back and chest out makes you look confident, and viewers are more likely to trust what you're saying about your products. Leaning forward slightly helps project your voice and conveys enthusiasm.

Or you can stand. Standing lets you move and breath more naturally, giving you more confidence and adding energy to your delivery.

#2 Gestures
ENHANCE YOUR MESSAGE

AKA "What do I do with my hands?"

Use hand gestures to highlight key points and add energy. Gestures above shoulder height really stand out. If you've ever seen a TED talk, you'll know what I mean. Bear in mind that too much movement can be distracting (and you risk becoming a meme!).

#3 Expressions
FACE VALUE

A variety of facial expressions can really spice up your streams. When you smile, it shows you're happy or approving and creates a friendly vibe. Frowning can help you show you're serious about something. Raising your eyebrows adds a fun touch, showing surprise or making things funny. Nodding shows you're listening and agreeing.

#4 Voice
SUPERCHARGED SPEECH

Voice modulation helps you emphasize key points, create contrast and generate interest and curiosity. Here's how:

- **Pitch**: Use high pitch for excitement and low pitch for seriousness.
- **Volume**: Speak louder to show confidence and softer for intimacy.
- **Tone**: Use a friendly tone for connection and a professional tone for credibility.
- **Speed**: Talk fast for energy and slow for clarity.
- **Pauses**: Use pauses to highlight key points and create suspense. Avoid too many or too long pauses.

DAY 8: RESPONDING TO COMMENTS & QUESTIONS IN REAL-TIME

Real-time interaction is the heartbeat of live streaming. Engaging with viewers by replying to their comments and questions, saying their names as you do so, helps to create open, dynamic, two-way conversations.

For your viewers, engagement makes them feel recognized. And for you, that engagement and recognition leads to more sales.

Note that a lot of viewers comment for the sake of commenting. You'll know what I mean if you've ever seen streams where the chat is just absolutely flooded and there's no time to read let alone respond to any comments. The best analogy I've heard for this is people at a wrestling match shouting out moves they wanna see the wrestlers do. They know it doesn't really have any impact, it's just crowd mentality and it's fun for them. If this happens to you, and you really don't want to miss any comments, your platform may offer "slow mode" or a spam filter. Otherwise, you can safely ignore the noise and just prioritize reading messages from regulars or users who have tagged you (@yourname).

Negative comments during live streams happen. But by being proactive, you can lower their impact and maintain a positive atmosphere. Number one: remain calm. Next, treat them as constructive criticism. This lets you address the comments in a constructive manner, and it makes the commenter feel heard. If viewers are being disrespectful or trolling, use your platform's moderation tools to filter out inappropriate remarks and manage the chat environment dynamically. Later on, you could hire an assistant who can help you moderate comments (see Day 16).

- Ask for your viewers' opinions and questions throughout the event.

- You don't have to respond to emojis sent as comments. It's fine if all you can do is send emojis back!

- Spot frequent commenters during your stream and call them out by name later. It's a simple way to boost conversions and keep viewers coming back.

SandyZ, that's a great point. Well spotted!

- Keep the comments section visible so everyone can join the conversation and see what's happening as it unfolds. This shows viewers that others are genuinely involved, which builds trust and encourages more participation.

- Stay tuned in to comments, like if someone asks to see a different view of a product. Include pauses in your show's timeline to address comments and answer questions. It shows you're listening and keeps the interaction lively.

DAY 8: MAKING YOUR AUDIENCE A COMMUNITY

Live events work best when you treat your entire audience like a single person. When you chat as if you're talking to one friend, you create a warm, welcoming space. Every comment gets a real reaction, and every name matters. You might say:

Hi, I am so glad you're here.

You'll feel so comfy in this.

When you want to build a real bond with your viewers and make each one feel like the only person in the room, remember this:

talk to one, not many

One of the greatest skills you can learn that'll help you in many areas of your life, not just in live selling, is making connections with individuals when speaking to groups of people. It's about how you can make a member of the audience feel as if you are speaking directly to them, and no one else.

And that's where *talk to one, not many* comes in. Always imagine you're talking to one person at a time, but only that you're in front of other people.

It feels so second nature to say, "How is everybody doing today?" and start with, "How many of you …" but you wouldn't say those in a one-on-one conversation.

So, instead:

talk as if you're addressing one person alone

Using the direct "you", you can say, "How are you doing today?" and start with, "Raise your hand if …" See the difference?

This approach works like a one-on-one chat, where every viewer feels seen and heard. By treating everything you say as a personal message, you build a warm, friendly space, which grows naturally into an inviting and close-knit community.

This advice was adopted from the words of multi-award-winning public speaker and creator of the Million Dollar Voice Formula Deborah Torres Patel, whose advice is:

"Public Speaking is just talking to one person at a time in front of other people."

DAY 8: IDEAS TO KEEP YOUR
LIVE EVENTS FRESH & FUN

You need to keep your live events engaging because viewers tend to lose focus quickly, especially online. Things like responding to comments and questions in real-time and making your audience a community are great for interaction. Adding visual variety, like switching between two camera angles or adding pre-recorded clips, is what'll capture and hold your audience's attention.

I know you won't use all these ideas now. Revisit them when you want to refresh your content.

VISUALLY FUN LIVE STREAM IDEAS

Play around with more than one video source. For example, having two camera angles that you can switch between; like one on your face and a secondary one for a wide shot or a close-up of your hands.

Share clips you've pre-recorded and edited. A good time to share these is the transition between segments. It gives you a breather and helps reset your viewer's attention span.

Switch to a real-time view of your computer screen. This is perfect for walking your viewers through a process where they need to see exactly what you're doing or demoing an answer to a question.

Put your phone on a selfie stick or gimbal and take a tour of your workspace, show a product up close or do part of your event from a different location.

Take it a step further and go shopping with your viewers. Show them your favorite stores and products and even pitch your items that would go really well with what you're showing.

PRO HACK

Unboxing is fun, but live packaging takes it to the next level. If you pack orders yourself, consider turning this task into an experience. It gives viewers a behind-the-scenes look at the process and shows how much attention and care you give every parcel. Give a shout out to the viewer you're packaging for. This makes them feel more involved in the experience.

Take on a viral challenge or make a ridiculous bet with your viewers. From eating something spicy or super sour candy to doing pushups or planks.

You can ask your viewers for suggestions, and the sillier the challenge, the better!

Do a live reaction video like the ones you see on YouTube where you watch and respond to a piece of content, like a viral video, trending news article, TV show clip, meme or even a product launch. Viewers love seeing real, unscripted emotions and hearing your thoughts on what you're watching.

Streaming is a great way to show off what makes you, *you*. Believe it or not, some streamers in China make tens of millions just by sharing their talents live. And no, you don't need Got Talent-level skills, just whatever makes your friends smile in real life can totally work online too. Here's two fun ways you can include this in your event naturally: "If we reach 100 viewers, I'll do a live dance." and "For every comment, I'll add a line to a live painting."

DAY 9: RUNNING AN EQUIPMENT SITE TEST

92 | PREPPING FOR THE SPOTLIGHT

On the day of every stream, double-check your setup. Create a plan for testing your gear and settings before hitting Go LIVE to make sure everything runs smoothly.

Check your camera and mic are working correctly. Use your streaming platform to preview the video and audio feed, checking for any issues.

Ensure you and any area where you'll display your products are well-lit.

Conduct a private test stream with your streaming platform to ensure that everything is working correctly before going live.

If possible, have someone watch your test stream and provide feedback on audio and video quality, background, lighting, camera angles, and visuals.

Check that your internet connection is stable, fast and can handle the demands of a live stream.

Choose a clean background. Reposition pictures and furniture, if needed, or use a green screen.

Unclutter your streaming space to avoid distractions.

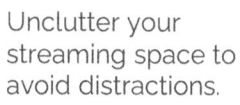

DAY 9: HANDLING TECHNICAL PROBLEMS

You ran a site test and everything worked beautifully. You're good to go, right? Nope. Live streaming is like the Wild West of digital content, a place where anything that can go wrong, will go wrong. Having a technical contingency plan takes the stress out of live streaming surprises, so you're prepped and ready to deal with (almost) anything.

COMMON PROBLEMS AND WHAT TO DO

	PROBLEM	WHAT IT IS	WHAT TO DO
INTERNET CONNECTION	Buffering	Your stream pauses or stutters.	Test your internet speed ahead of time, connect via ethernet if you can, disconnect other devices on your network and close unnecessary apps to keep your bandwidth free.
	Frequent drops	An unstable internet connection and inconsistent upload speeds can interrupt your live stream.	In addition to the above steps, check if your internet service provider (ISP) is having issues in your area. Consider having a backup plan like a mobile hotspot to switch over to to get you through to the end of your event.
AUDIO	Lagging voice	Your voice might lag behind the video or it sounds strange or unclear.	Check that all cables are fully connected. Next check your microphone settings against what your platform suggests. You might need to reconnect your mic and restart your computer.

PROBLEM	WHAT IT IS	WHAT TO DO
VIDEO		
Frozen or stuttering video	Video appears jerky, stuttering or freezes completely.	Lower the video resolution or bitrate, if needed, and ensure your device and streaming software are up to date and working smoothly. If you don't know how to check and edit your encoder settings to match platform requirements, check the help center for the platform and your encoder app/tool.
Video drops completely	Your viewers can hear you but no longer see you.	In addition to the above steps, check that your computer can keep up. The high demand on your processor and graphics card from live streaming can be too much and cause overheating, especially when you have other devices demanding resources and power from your computer. If a restart doesn't fix the problem, you have three choices: 1. Use less devices. 2. Upgrade your system. 3. Use browser-based live streaming software.

Always check if an issue is only affecting one viewer or everyone. If just one, then the issue is likely on their side, and you can advise that viewer to drop off and rejoin the session.

When troubleshooting a live stream issue on your side, stay composed and guide your viewers through the process by providing updates. Try the fastest solutions first. But if that fails, a computer restart usually solves most issues. So, if you need to restart the session, explain what's happening and how your viewers can easily rejoin.

DAY 9: PRACTICING TRANSITIONS IN DEMOS

Smooth transitions between product demos keep your event flowing naturally and avoid making it all sound like a sales pitch. It's easier said than done and takes a bit of practice. So, here are some tips with practical examples you can use till you find your feet with moving from one product to the next.

CONNECT PRODUCTS WITH A HOOK

Find a storyline or use case that connects two items:
- *"This bag looks great with the wallet I just showed you."*
- *"Earlier, I talked about cold weather gear. This is the layering piece that ties it all together."*

SCRIPT TRANSITIONAL PHRASES

Prepare 10–15 short transition phrases that naturally guide viewers from one item to the next, swapping keywords depending on what you're selling:
- *"Now if you loved that, wait till you see this next one!"*
- *"Speaking of keeping things organized, here's something that takes it to the next level."*
- *"Let's switch gears. This one's for all the coffee lovers watching!"*

CREATE A SIGNATURE TRANSITION STYLE

Make your transitions part of your brand voice; funny, stylish, sassy or whatever depending on your vibe:
- *"And just like that..."*
- *"Okay, friends, here's the real showstopper!"*
- *"Let's ease into the next one. It's my softest tank yet"*

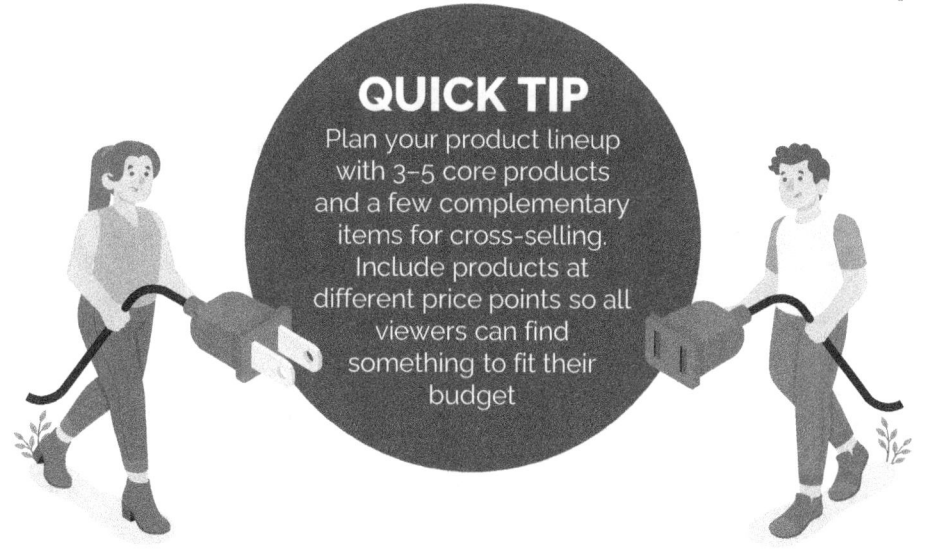

QUICK TIP
Plan your product lineup with 3-5 core products and a few complementary items for cross-selling. Include products at different price points so all viewers can find something to fit their budget

USE VISUAL OR PHYSICAL CUES

Your transitions can be physical and visual, not just verbal:
- Hold the next item partially in frame as you're wrapping up the first. Use a hook phrase like, *"And just wait until you see what I've got next..."*
- While talking about an item, hang a matching item behind you or place it on the table, then casually reach for it as you finish your point.

GROUP PRODUCTS INTO STORY SETS

Build "mini-collections" so one item naturally leads into another. Think in outfits, emotions, routines, activities, themes, gameplay strategies and so on:
- *"The LBD is a classic, no doubt. But if you're feeling playful, this jewel-toned party dress adds just the right splash of color to your wardrobe."*
- *"You've got your fortress with the Ironhold card set, but what if you could strike first? This Swiftblade series is all about speed and precision."*

USE AUDIENCE CUES

If viewers are asking about features or a related product, use that as a natural transition:
- *"mary26, I see you asking about matching covers and protectors. Let me grab those next!"*
- *"I see a comment about fit. I'll cover that while I show you the next shirt."*

DAY 10: GUESS WHAT? YOU'RE GOING LIVE TOMORROW!

Sorry if you hadn't figured that out already, but there's method to my madness. By waiting until the last minute to tell you, I've spared you from getting bogged down in unnecessary stress because oftentimes, the best events happen when you jump in without overthinking.

Instead, you can channel your energy into preparing quickly and confidently, keeping the momentum fresh and your excitement high. Sometimes, spontaneity is the secret sauce to delivering a truly authentic and engaging live selling event!

That being said, no-one just goes live and hopes for the best. So, today you're gonna create buzz about the event by giving your social followers a reason to tune in.

Don't worry if you haven't got products yet or your setup isn't complete. Use this as an opportunity to connect with your followers on a personal level. Share the journey of getting your live selling setup together or give them a behind-the-scenes look. Building rapport now will make your future sessions even stronger.

So go ahead and share a teaser on social media and tell your community where, when and how to connect with you on your first live event. How exciting!

DAY 10: INVITE YOUR FRIENDS & FAMILY

Inviting your friends and family to join your first livestream on social media tomorrow is a great way to kick things off. And lots of sellers and small businesses actually get their first sales from someone they know.

The hardest parts for you, as they were for me, are 1.) asking loved ones for their support because you never want to make someone feel obliged and 2.) charging them full price for any products they order. But my business growth and exposure are thanks to my amazing friends and family who have placed orders, shared with their connections and posted on social media when I was first starting out.

To make things easier on you and anyone you share an emotional connection with, let them know about your plan to start live selling and that you have your first livestream soon. Plant the seed in their minds and let it grow. That way, you're just reaching out to let them know what you're doing, but you're not pushing them to do anything or buy anything. Not everyone will be your cheerleader and that's ok.

TIPS ON SELLING TO FRIENDS & FAMILY

You're totally allowed to have friends and family join your stream, buy your products and leave reviews. But they must willingly shop at your store and leave genuine reviews, otherwise things get a tad shady.

To keep things above board, avoid orders coming in from anyone sharing the same internet connection and shipping address. And especially not from your or a shared payment account.

If someone did buy from you and wants to leave a review, ask them not to mention you personally or their relationship to you in their review.

WHY IT'S GOOD TO INVITE F&F

Having familiar faces at your event can provide moral support, which can be incredibly reassuring, especially while you're new to live selling.

Friends and family can help you reach a wider audience by sharing your live event with their networks.

People are more likely to trust and engage with you if they see others you know vouching for you.

Your close circle can offer valuable real-time feedback during and after the event: what worked well and what could be improved.

Friends and family might be more inclined to purchase your products. Their enthusiasm can be contagious, encouraging other viewers to buy as well.

A supportive audience can create a positive and engaging atmosphere, making it more enjoyable for both you and your viewers.

YOU TOTALLY GOT THIS

Just look at your progress! Ready to go live?

DAY 6:

❏ Decide what to include in your live events.

❏ Create an event timeline, shaped to suit you.

❏ Prepare key selling points for your demo.

DAY 7:

❏ Overcome shyness by being yourself.

❏ Develop a hosting persona.

❏ Build confidence in front of the camera.

DAY 8:

❏ Prepare interactive elements for live events.

❏ Have a plan for responding to live comments.

❏ Know how to create an engaging community.

DAY 9:

❑ Run an equipment site test.

❑ Make a plan to deal with technical issues.

❑ Practice transitions in your product demo.

DAY 10:

❑ Get the word out about your event tomorrow.

❑ Invite your friends and family.

GOING LIVE

DAY 11: PRE-SHOW CHECKLIST

Live selling moves fast, so being prepared is important. A little glitch or pause can mess up your show and lose you sales. That's why a checklist before going live is a good idea.

CHECKLIST

A live selling pre-show checklist should include product preparation (checking stock, displaying items attractively), technical setup (camera, lighting, microphone, internet connection), script outlining key points, promotional strategy (social media posts, notifications), audience engagement plan (questions, giveaways), and a final run-through; making sure to address any potential issues before going live.

Here's a list of essentials you can use to create your own checklist and ensure your live stream runs flawlessly.

ESSENTIALS FOR A SUCCESSFUL STREAM

PRODUCT INVENTORY

- ❏ Select and lay out the products you want to sell, in the order you want to show them.
- ❏ Make sure all the items are uploaded to your inventory with the quantities you or your supplier has available.

TECHNICAL SETUP

- ❏ Ensure your camera is positioned correctly, with good lighting and focus.
- ❏ Check microphone quality and volume levels.
- ❏ Run an internet connection test for speed and stability.
- ❏ Go over the technical contingency plan you created on Day 9.

HEAD AND BODY

- ❏ Thoroughly review your script, including intro, product demos (features, benefits and key selling points) and Q&A sections.
- ❏ Get dressed and camera ready.
- ❏ Drink some water and nip to the loo.

SOCIAL MEDIA PROMOTION

- ❏ Have you posted teasers, reminders and live links across all your relevant platforms?
- ❏ Get any visual aids (graphics, slides or product images) ready.

PRE-SHOW RUN-THROUGH

- ❏ Do a complete practice run through of your entire live stream.

DRESS REHEARSAL FOR A PRIVATE AUDIENCE

If you can, ask a friend to connect to a private livestream and do a dress rehearsal with cameras, products and everything. Tell them to post questions and place dummy orders in real-time.

DAY 11: ENJOYING YOUR FIRST LIVE SALE

Go live.

Have fun.

Enjoy it.

QUICK TIP

It's your first live selling event, so mistakes are natural. Focus on connecting with your audience. They'll appreciate your authenticity, and every stumble is a chance to improve for next time. You've learned enough to start strong. So, dive in and give it your best shot!

DAY 11: POST-SHOW ANALYSIS & LESSONS LEARNED

Did your first live show leave you tongue-tied and overwhelmed? You're in good company. 99% of YouTubers and live streamers feel the same way starting out. Social anxiety is an absolute killer, but with time and practice, it really does improve.

Live selling has been a blast for me, and I hope it becomes that for you too! I've been streaming for years, and I still get nervous, but the excitement of hitting the Go LIVE button wins every time.

Right now, you're swirling with a mix of adrenaline, relief and second-guessing. That's completely normal. Before diving into the nitty-gritty of what could've gone better, take a moment to celebrate what went right.

CELEBRATE THE WINS

Number one, give yourself a pat on the back for the courage it took to go live for the first time. Many people never make it past their nerves, but you did! Whether it was smooth sailing or a bit bumpy, simply showing up and putting yourself out there is a huge achievement. And even if your audience was small, each viewer is a step toward something greater.

Think about the moments where you caught your viewer's attention. Could be a small smile, a simple nod or even a quick response. These little interactions are proof that you can spark engagement and build relationships.

What else did you enjoy?

SCARY INTRODUCTIONS

Something I hear a lot from sellers starting out with live is feeling awkward introducing themselves at the start of each show. If that happened to you today, don't fret; it's very common. The problem with an introduction is it's the first thing you say and if it feels awkward, you feel flustered straight away and it's hard to get over that feeling. If you want to keep an intro, make it simple like "Hey, Olivia here." and then get right into what you want to talk about that day. Or even don't introduce yourself at all. The point is, do what makes you feel comfortable.

CAUGHT OFF GUARD

Unexpected questions, technical glitches and moments where you just drew a blank. Surprises like these are the reality of live selling but they're also where growth happens. If something happened that threw you off script, celebrate the fact that you kept going and take it as a chance to learn. Moments like these let you think about how you can handle similar moments more smoothly next time.

> **PRO HACK**
> Just as you are building a community around you, so too should you join a community of like-minded live sellers. Facebook groups or even subreddits are great for connecting with others who've been through similar challenges and can provide emotional and technical support.

DAYS 1-10

You learned a heck of a lot up to this point. Now think about what actually happened in your livestream because reading about something is NOT the same thing as doing it. Walk with your new experience back through the first half of this book and you'll find things that make more sense now and how you can be better prepared for next time.

When you're ready, move on to Day 12 and 13 with confidence, where you'll learn about analyzing your performance with data.

DO LOTS MORE LIVE EVENTS
AND KEEP GETTING BETTER

Ok, time to calm things down. Your first show is in the bag, I know it was terrifying but it's over now, so take a deep breath and relax. I also know that many of you reading this book have already done a live show before. The following next steps apply to all, no matter what boat you're in.

This book is all about preparing you for your first "earning" live event at the end of 21 days. Sidenote: the days don't have to be consecutive. That means you've got at least 10 days of perfecting your craft before the big event. Here's a good way to make the most of that time:

- ❑ Process any orders you received from today's event (see Day 12).
- ❑ Continue reading. The rest of the book is less about action and more about learning how to improve as a live seller.
- ❑ Go live again as many times as you can before the big event, trying different strategies you've learned.
- ❑ Set a date and start building buzz around your big event.

YOU ROCK!

Enjoying the book? I'd love your feedback! Leave your review by heading to your Amazon Orders page.

Thanks a bunch!

YOU TOTALLY GOT THIS

Wow, your first livestream in the bag! High five!

DAY 11:

❑ Create a pre-show checklist.

❑ Have fun doing your first live selling event.

❑ Revisit Days 1-10 with a fresh perspective.

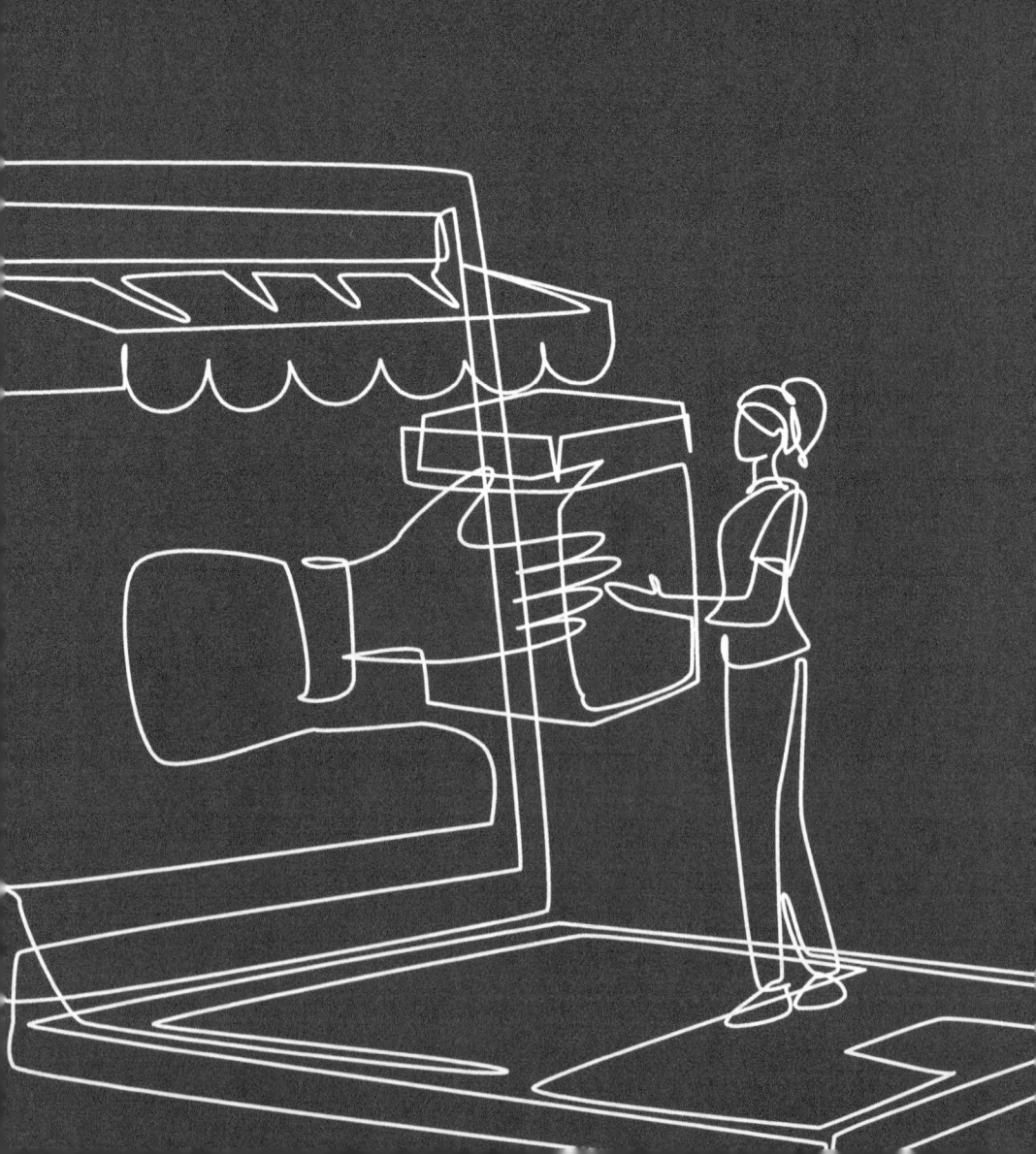

SHIP ORDERS & ANALYSIS

SHIP ORDERS & ANALYSIS
DAY 12: PROCESSING YOUR FIRST
ORDERS

If you made a big fat zero number of orders from yesterday's live event, then welcome to the club. The vast majority of people don't make a single sale during their first live selling experience, and that's perfectly normal. Think of it as a crucial first step, not a failure!

Even without sales, yesterday was incredibly valuable. You gained experience speaking on camera and with your viewers in real-time.

But if you did happen to make sales, **congratulations!** That's wonderful. Now it's time to get those orders packed and shipped.

> **QUICK TIP**
> Keep proper records so you can easily determine income vs profit earned from orders and running costs when it comes time to do your income tax return. Aim to keep records for at least 5 years.

1 Go through each order and make sure everything looks right, like items, sizes, addresses, customization requests, etc. If anything's unclear, send your customer a quick email.

Even if you're using dropshipping or some other service that takes and ships orders for you, you should still double check your orders all look ok, especially for the first wee while until you can trust it all works as expected.

2 Gather all the items for each order. Give them a quick once-over to make sure they're perfect. Look for scratches, smudges and missing pieces. Then wrap each item up nice and snug so they arrive safe and sound.

Before sealing the package, pop in a packing slip or handwritten "Thank you!" It helps make the experience feel more personal.

MANAGING EXPECTATIONS

Be realistic about shipping times, especially if you're hand-packing everything. For instance, don't promise overnight delivery if you can't do that. Clearly state your processing timelines within order confirmation emails. **Under-promise and over-deliver if possible!**

And if there's a delay like stock issues, reach out to the affected customer immediately. A quick, honest explanation goes a long way. Say something like, "Hey, just wanted to let you know there's a slight delay due to [add reason here]. I expect to ship your order on [add new date here]. Sorry for the delay. Thanks a lot for your patience." Read over the page to learn more about handling shipping (and returns).

3 Print out shipping labels and compare against the address listed on the order. Pick a carrier that works for you (price and speed are key). Drop off your packages or schedule a pickup.

When you know the tracking numbers (from the carrier or your fulfillment partner), send them to your customers ASAP.

4 A few days after delivery, send your customers a quick email asking if everything arrived okay and if they're happy with their purchases. Encourage them to leave a review.

If you're using dropshipping or another service like Fulfilled by Amazon (FBA), keep a close eye on customer feedback about quality of their items received and speed of shipments.

DAY 12: HANDLING
SHIPPING & RETURNS

You did your best getting those packages to your viewers quickly (and hopefully with minimal headaches). But packages sometimes get lost, damaged or delayed. It happens.

On the flip side, it's an amazing feeling when a product you've lovingly packed and shipped arrived early and in perfect condition. But then you get a return request, and that happy feeling turns sour. And the more sales you make, the more returns you'll get. Returns are one of the toughest parts. They cost you money, create headaches and can leave you feeling like you've disappointed someone. How you handle these situations is crucial.

5 If a viewer reaches out to you because a product is taking longer than expected to arrive, reach out to the carrier as soon as possible to start a search. In the meantime, keep the viewer updated every step of the way. If needed, offer solutions, whether it's reshipping the order (if your stock allows ofc), issuing a refund (see the next page) or providing store credit (if your platform supports it).

6 Sometimes packages don't show up because you were given the wrong address (or you wrote the wrong address, oops!).

If a package is returned to you due to an incorrect address, contact the viewer to confirm the correct address. Offer to reship the package. It's up to you if you want them to pay extra shipping costs or not, but if it was your fault, reship it without charging them extra.

KEEPING VIEWERS HAPPY (EVEN WHEN THINGS GO WRONG)

Refunds. They're a reality of running any business. It doesn't matter if it's damaged goods, incorrect items, late delivery, customer dissatisfaction or simply a change of heart, dealing with refunds is a downer, like that person is mad at you personally.

The silver lining is that you can turn this negative experience into a positive one, giving such great customer service that can lead to positive reviews and more business. Always look for ways to go the extra mile. You could offer a small gift along with a replacement or a discount code for a future purchase. Small things like these can help smooth things over and encourage viewers to buy from you again.

> Sure, great customer service is important but don't be afraid to push back if you believe a viewer is abusing your returns policy, making fraudulent claims or if the request is well beyond your stated returns window.

7 If a viewer requests a refund, don't leave them hanging, hoping they'll change their mind. Respond within 24 hours, letting them know you got the request and are working on it. A simple "We're sorry to hear you're not satisfied with your purchase and we're happy to help resolve this issue." goes a long way. From here, you can start investigating the issue, trying to understand the reason for the refund. Ask for details, photos (if applicable) and any relevant information.

Now you can offer a solution. Depending on the situation, you might offer a replacement, an exchange, a store credit or a full refund. Let them choose the option that works best for them and process it quickly. If you're using dropshipping or another service like FBA, follow the process as per their return agreement.

DAY 12: GAIN VIEWER LOYALTY WITH
GREAT SERVICE

Customer service ranks among the top reasons people stay loyal to their favorite brands. It's more important than price. Strong customer service beyond a live selling event leaves viewers feeling valued, not just sold to. And showing your viewers that you care about their needs and satisfaction turns one-time buyers into long-term supporters.

FACTORS THAT EARN AND KEEP CUSTOMER LOYALTY TO A BRAND

3. CUSTOMER SERVICE
4. SHOPPING EXPERIENCE
2. VALUE FOR MONEY
1. PRODUCT QUALITY
5. PRODUCT PRICES

Word-of-mouth is gold. People not only trust recommendations from friends and family, but they're also more likely to spend more. So, if you focus on top-notch service, it leads to delighted customers who help grow your brand simply by sharing their positive experiences. And you save money on advertising, yay!

3 PILLARS OF GREAT CUSTOMER SERVICE

BEING PROACTIVE

Be the first to reach out and address viewer needs before they arise.

IDEAS:
- Send personalized thank yous to everyone who joined your live event and those who purchased.
- Follow up to address any unanswered questions.
- Process all your orders promptly.
- For any holdups, reach out to viewers individually.
- Keep an eye on what viewers say and do. It helps you spot potential hiccups early and smooth things out.

FAST ANSWERS

Quick problem-solving keeps customers happy and ensures they return.

IDEAS:
- Have in-depth expertise in your product, service, order fulfillment, payment options and so on, so you're ready to respond instantly to concerns.
- Send out new products first and deal with the faulty, returned ones afterward.
- Provide easy refund options.
- Aim to answer support questions and email enquiries within 24 hours.

CHANNEL VARIETY

Give viewers access to support in a way that works best for them.

IDEAS:
- Provide real-time chat support for immediate responses to questions or concerns.
- Use platforms like WhatsApp or Facebook Messenger for personal communication.
- Let viewers post questions publicly on your socials so anyone with the same concern can see the answer.

DAY 13: TRACKING THE KEY METRICS

Measuring success is a must for any business. For live selling, crucial metrics act as your roadmap, showing what's going well, what needs attention and where you can grow the most. With clear data, you can make wiser decisions and get better results.

You'll learn about analytics tools in the next pages. For now, here are the key metrics you should focus on for analyzing the success of your live selling events. And no, sales alone don't capture the full picture.

CORE METRICS FOR SUCCESS

	METRIC	WHAT IT IS	WHY IT'S VALUABLE
VIEWERSHIP & DURATION	Total Views	How many viewers tuned in to your live session.	Provides a general overview of your reach.
	Peak Concurrent Viewers	The highest number of viewers tuned in at any given time.	Helps you identify the most engaging moments of your event when viewer attention was at its peak.
	Average Watch Time	The average amount of time viewers spent watching your event.	A longer average watch time means viewers are finding your content valuable and are more likely to make a purchase.
ENGAGEMENT	Chat Activity	The volume of comments, questions and messages exchanged.	High chat activity indicates that viewers are actively engaged with your content and are eager to interact with the host and other participants.
	Reactions & Emotes	How many likes, hearts, emojis and other reactions that viewers used.	These visual cues can help you gauge audience sentiment.

	METRIC	WHAT IT IS	WHY IT'S VALUABLE
SALES AND REVENUE	**Total Sales Revenue**	The total amount of revenue generated.	This is the ultimate metric for measuring the financial success of your event.
	Conversion Rate	The percentage of viewers who made a purchase.	A higher conversion rate suggests that your content is compelling, your products are appealing and your call to action is effective.
	Average Order Value (AOV)	The average amount of money spent per order. It's the total revenue divided by the number of orders.	This metric can help you identify viewer preferences as well as opportunities for upselling or cross-selling related products.
	Click-Through Rate (CTR)	The percentage of viewers who clicked on a product link or other call to action.	A high CTR means your product placement is effective and viewers want to learn more about your products. A CTR of 2% or higher is considered good.
	Add-to-Cart Rate	The percentage of viewers who added a product to their shopping cart.	Keep in mind that not every viewer who adds an item to their cart will purchase it. Cross-reference this data with Abandoned Cart Rate.
	Return Rate	The percentage of sold items that are returned.	In the ecommerce world, a return rate below 5% is good.

Most (probably all) of these metrics won't be super useful at first. But by regularly analyzing these core metrics, you'll begin to spot trends and patterns emerging in your performance, letting you improve your future live events and product offerings to meet viewer demand.

And when analysis becomes second nature, you can begin looking at metrics like individual viewer data, locations, device types, and so on, which help you segment viewers for a more personalized approach.

124 | SHIP ORDERS & ANALYSIS

DAY 13: FINDING YOUR EDGE WITH
ANALYTICS TOOLS

With data on key metrics, you can tap into detailed insights that reveal exactly where your live events shine and where a little fine-tuning can make all the difference. The challenge is zeroing in on those golden metrics and making sense of them all. That's where analytics tools come in.

PLATFORM BUILT-IN ANALYTICS TOOLS

When it comes to tracking your key live event metrics, the most convenient tool at your disposal is the integrated analytics tool of your chosen platforms. Most live shopping platforms like YouTube, TikTok Shop and Shopify have analytics you can use at no extra charge.

The great thing about using built-in analytics tools is they often come with pre-built reports and dashboards for exactly the kinds of things that users like you need them for. And getting familiar with them is easy.

For example, TikTok Shop has its integrated analytics tool within its Seller Center. It lets you to spot trends in your key metrics live as well as across different time periods using a range of easy-to-read graphs, charts and reports.

TIP: Compare different periods to track how well you're doing compared to the previous month and year.

INTEGRATING THIRD-PARTY ANALYTICS

Built-in analytics tools are a great resource, and they may be all you'll ever need. But what if you …
- want to dig deeper into the data?
- want to customize what to track and how it's reported?
- host your store off-platform, like on your own website?

Of course, you'll have to pay for the privilege, but in addition to the list above, many specialized analytics services also provide advanced competitor analysis and market insights that free built-in tools simply can't match. For example, platforms like Kalodata, Rival IQ, Emplifi and EchoTik not only monitor your own performance but also offer side-by-side comparisons with key competitors. This level of intelligence lets you capitalize on emerging trends, tailor your content strategy and fine-tune your live selling tactics based on what's working in your niche.

ONE ~~RING~~ TOOL TO RULE THEM ALL

Spend your money on third-party analytics when you want to elevate your game. Like if there comes a time when you host live events and sell products on multiple platforms, say TikTok, YouTube and Shopify. That's when juggling all the separate analytics tools can quickly get overwhelming, and that's where third-party tools shine. They integrate data from all your platforms into one clean interface, so you can spot trends across platforms and optimize your strategy holistically.

PRO HACK

Dive deeper into exit points. Exit points are the specific moments where viewership drops. Ask "At what point are viewers leaving your event?" and "Were they turned off by a particular product, a technical glitch or a lull in engagement?" By analyzing exit points, you can identify potential problem areas and fix them for next time.

YOU TOTALLY GOT THIS

The more you learn the more you'll earn!

DAY 12:

❏ Process any orders you got from your event.

❏ Make a plan to deal with shipping issues and returns.

❏ Commit to giving great customer service.

DAY 13:

❏ Define the key metrics you want to track.

❏ Choose an analytics tool to measure your progress.

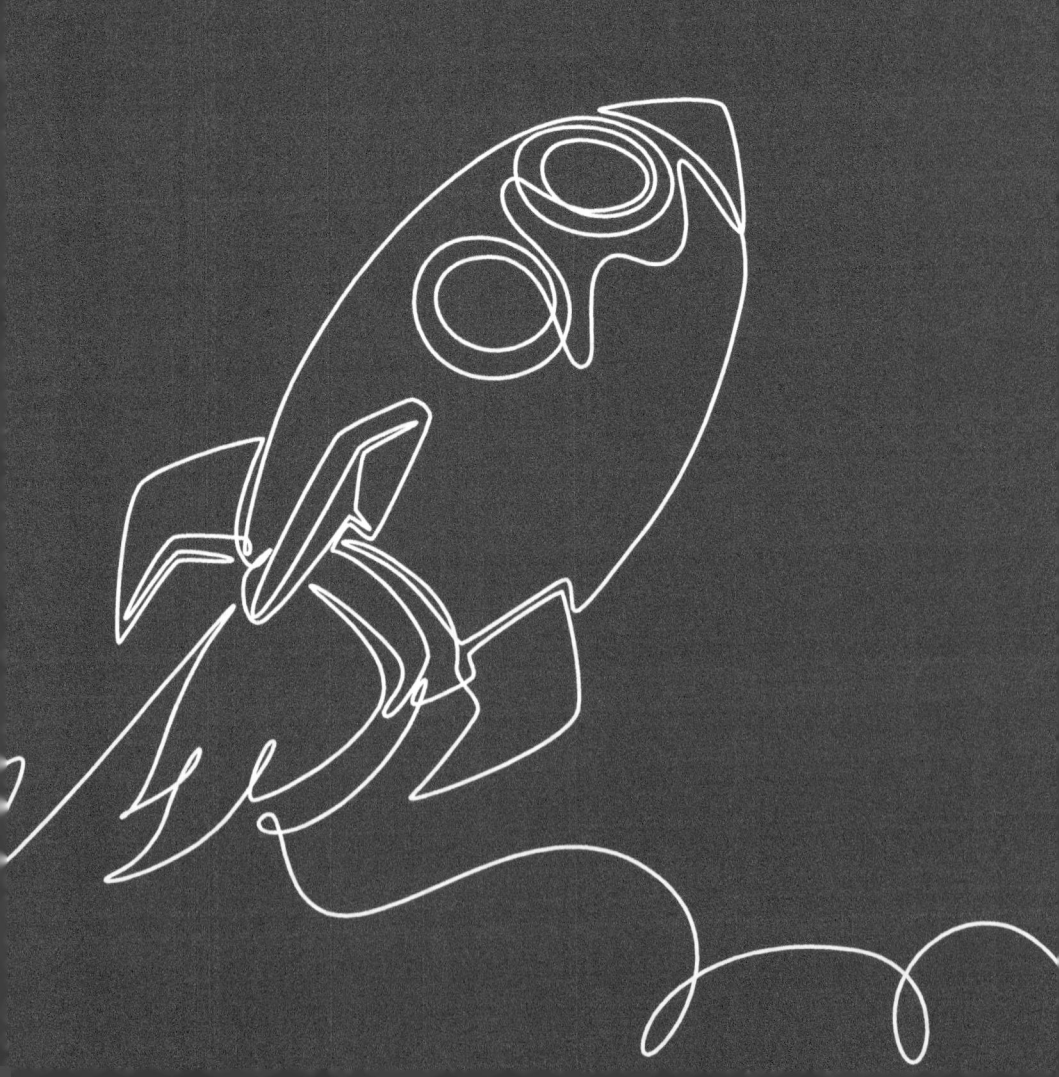

SCALING YOUR OPERATIONS

DAY 14: HOW TO USE
A/B TESTING

A/B testing is a way of comparing two or more versions of something to find out which one works best. For instance, you can test the length and format of your live event to see which draws more viewers, engagement and conversions. Experimenting in this way helps you make choices based on real data, making your streams the best they can be and maximizing your return on investment.

IDENTIFYING WHAT WORKS AND WHAT WORKS **BETTER**

DEFINE YOUR GOAL AND HYPOTHESIS

Ask yourself:
What's the outcome I'm aiming for?
What do I believe will make it happen?

Think of A/B testing as a recipe experiment. Your goal is the dish you want to perfect, and your hypothesis is the new ingredient you believe will improve the flavor.

Let's use the following as an example:

- **GOAL:** Higher conversions
- **HYPOTHESIS:** Adding a final call to action will increase sales

DESIGN YOUR EXPERIMENT

Sticking with the recipe theme (sorry, I love food!), you'll test two versions by tweaking the ingredients (variables) and measure the results (metrics). Be sure to choose the right number of taste-testers (sample size) and enough time to cook your results (duration).

Now ask:
What are the elements that I want to test?
What metrics do I need to measure?
How many viewers do I need to test each version?
How long do I need to run the test?

- **VARIABLES**: Asking and not asking viewers at the end of my event to buy my product.
- **METRICS**: Number of clicks to the product sales page.
- **SAMPLE SIZE**: At least 20 viewers.
- **DURATION**: Five events for each variable.

RUN YOUR A/B TESTS

Keep these two points in mind when running your tests:
- If you're running multiple A/B tests, make sure they don't overlap or influence each other. Keep one variable per experiment to maintain clarity in your data.
- If you notice a major issue or clear trends early, make adjustments as needed or stop the test.

A NEW BASELINE

Act on your findings, updating your strategy with the top-performing version, then experiment with other elements.

DAY 14: INTRODUCING NEW PRODUCTS ON DEMAND

Knowing what sells is half the battle. And thanks to the customer feedback and analytics at your fingertips, you've got a clear picture of what products your viewers love. Now you can take those winning products and branch out, introducing new products that complement or improve on or give more variety to what your viewers want.

DIVE INTO YOUR BESTSELLERS

Never launch a new product on a whim. Understanding the "why" behind the success of your bestselling items is always the best first step.

What Viewers Think

The reactions and comments you get during your live events or on your social posts tell you so much about what products your viewers are into. Whether it's glowing reviews or excitement over certain items, this feedback is your guide to expanding your product lineup

What Viewers Do

Analyze your sales data to identify your top-selling items. Doing things like comparing the price point, design and function against not-so-popular products, as well as dissecting data from A/B tests, can tell you what makes your bestsellers so well-liked.

BRAINSTORM IDEAS FOR NEW PRODUCTS

Once you've pinpointed your popular items, think about variations of new products that are similar but offer a unique twist or cater to different needs of your viewers.

More Premium Versions
Can a bestseller be made with higher-grade materials, more exclusive or advanced features or be customized in some valuable way?

Budget Choices
Can you offer a simplified version of a popular product but at a lower price point, focusing on essential features while maintaining quality?

Related Products
Are there any accessories or matching items that go nicely with your bestsellers? This can create cross-selling and bundle opportunities (see next page).

Different Styles or Features
Does your supplier offer your bestseller in different colors, designs, functionalities or even limited-edition versions that viewers who are on the fence might like?

> Live selling is a fantastic space to experiment, so don't worry if a new product doesn't land how you'd imagined. Keep testing, and when a new product sells well, invest time trying to understand why.

DAY 14: INTRODUCING CROSS-SELL & UPSELL

CROSS-SELLING

Cross-selling is like when Amazon shows products that are "Frequently Bought Together". The products aren't the same, but they are related, like a matching necklace for a dress or a yoga mat for yoga pants.

You're helping your viewers discover products that work perfectly with what they're already buying. **For you, it increases the overall sale and exposes more of your products to viewers.**

Be careful though because doing it too often and giving too many suggestions can lead to decision fatigue. And if not done carefully, the products you suggest may not match their needs.

UPSELLING

Upselling is all about showing viewers why a more expensive option might be worth it. Maybe it's a pricier item with more features, like a thicker yoga mat, or a bundle that combines several must-haves into one deal, like a simple pendant necklace that includes matching earrings.

Upselling encourages your viewers to spend more, making it a good tactic for premium items that give you higher profit margins. Your viewers also feel more satisfied with the enhanced value of their purchase.

Don't be too aggressive with upselling as it can make viewers feel pressured, driving them away.

DAY 14: INTRODUCING PRODUCT BUNDLES

ESSENTIALS

An **Essentials** bundle includes key items that viewers frequently purchase but not usually together. Buying socks is boring. But a whole, coordinated gym outfit with shirt, shorts and socks? For a skincare seller, you could offer a basics bundle with cleanser, toner and moisturizer.

This kind of bundle helps your viewers get everything they need in one purchase, making their decision-making process easier. You can also price the bundle slightly lower than if they bought each item separately, increasing perceived value. You'll save money on shipping costs, so your profit margin shouldn't be too affected.

EXCLUSIVE

An **Exclusive** bundle brings together a selection of products but is only available for a short period. Imagine wet-weather workout gear for winter or a travel-themed self-care package before the start of the summer holiday season.

In addition to the benefits of selling essentials bundles, this kind of exclusive bundle creates urgency, pushing your viewers to act fast before the bundle disappears. It also helps you introduce new products in a way that feels special and exciting.

DAY 15: RUNNING CONTESTS & GIVEAWAYS

Giveaways are a blast for viewers. They add a fun, interactive element that makes people want to stay tuned and participate. But it takes more than just buying a gift card and picking a winner. Careful planning will get the results you want.

There are four moving parts to a successful contest.

STEP 1: DEFINE YOUR CONTEST OBJECTIVES

Start by setting clear goals for your contest. Think about what you want to achieve from your giveaway, whether it's generating leads, boosting sales, increasing brand awareness, gaining more social media followers, engaging your audience, driving traffic to your website, or gathering content created by viewers. With these goals in mind, you can plan a campaign that supports and achieves them.

QUICK TIP

You'll attract a mixed crowd to your contest. And lots of likes and participants are great, but if they aren't your target audience, you won't see any return on investment. To fix this, tailor your contest to appeal to your ideal audience.

STEP 2: PICK THE PERFECT PRIZE

Choose a prize that appeals to your target audience and aligns with your brand. Consider your budget, find something valuable but affordable, or free, like your own products (digital or physical) or your services. Highlight its value to attract the right crowd. You might get fewer participants, but they'll be more likely to become loyal customers. You could even let the winner pick a prize from some options.

STEP 3: DESIGN YOUR CONTEST

Decide how and when your content will run during your live stream. You could ask viewers to comment with a hashtag to enter, then pick a random winner at the very end, for example. This way, it's simple, engaging and keeps viewers tuned in for a chance to win.

There are even tools out there that make contests super easy to set up and run. Plus, they ensure fair entry rules, so you can focus on the fun stuff.

Remember to follow platform rules and local laws.

STEP 4: PROMOTE YOUR CONTEST EVERYWHERE

Get the word out far and wide for maximum engagement!

- Create a landing page for your contest.
- Send an email blast to your list.
- Promote on all social channels.
- Feature it on your website/blog.
- Invest in social media ads for a bigger reach. (if you can).

DAY 15: STRATEGIES FOR REWARDING LOYALTY

The US is home to more than three billion loyalty program memberships. That's ten for every person living there. It's clear these programs are woven into our daily lives and are especially popular with high-earners.

The world of loyalty programs is so mainstream, it's almost boring. But in a good way! People know the drill: points, perks and rewards. So, instead of feeling like a sales gimmick, when you roll out a loyalty program, your viewers recognize it as a standard offering.

ELEMENTS OF AN EFFECTIVE LOYALTY PROGRAM

EXCLUSIVE
Special perks add value; rewarding everyone takes that away

ATTRACTIVE
The best rewards are those so enticing that viewers can't resist putting in the effort to earn them

EFFORTLESS
Joining the program must be quick and hassle-free

WIN-WIN
A balanced program means viewers get enticing rewards while you meet your business goals

REPEATABLE
A predictable rewards system keeps customers motivated to participate again and again

BRANDABLE
Your rewards should feel personal and reflect the unique value that draws viewers to you

Loyalty programs are so varied they can be shaped and sized to suit any business model and customer base. There's a points system, but you'll need a platform or tools that support it. There's a paid subscription model, but you'll need to provide enough value in return for their money. There's also a multi-tired system where you segment your viewers, meaning there's a lot more for you to manage.

In the end, there are two strategies that work well for live selling and meet many elements of an effective loyalty program.

A **PERKS PROGRAM** gives members-only rewards like free shipping or discounts for specific actions, like registering early for live events or spending over a certain amount.

☑ EXCLUSIVE
☑ ATTRACTIVE
☑ EFFORTLESS
☑ WIN-WIN
☑ REPEATABLE
☐ BRANDABLE

A **REFERRAL PROGRAM** rewards your viewers for spreading the word as well as the family and friends they refer. You'll remember from Day 12 that people trust personal recommendations and tend to spend more.

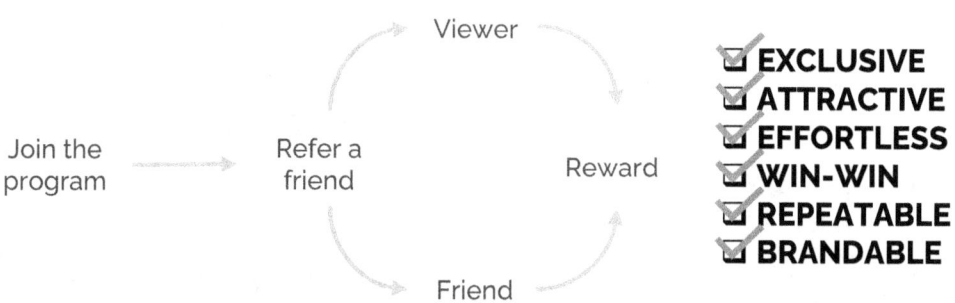

☑ EXCLUSIVE
☑ ATTRACTIVE
☑ EFFORTLESS
☑ WIN-WIN
☑ REPEATABLE
☑ BRANDABLE

DAY 15: COLLABORATING WITH INFLUENCERS

Teaming up with fellow influencers is a powerful way to tap into new audiences, strengthen your community and spark higher levels of interaction.

WAYS TO COLLABORATE

- Host live events together, remotely or in-person.
- Pitch an interview or guest speaker role to an influencer.
- Partner on a campaign or project, like a giveaway or contest.
- Promote each other's content on each other's accounts.

BENEFITS OF COLLABORATION

- You both get access to new audiences and followers through your networks.
- Collaborative content often generates more comments, likes and shares.
- Working with other respected influencers can boost your own reputation.

TIPS FOR SUCCESSFUL COLLABORATION

- Collaborate with influencers whose values and content align with or complement your own.
- Offer something meaningful to your collaborator and their audience.
- Chat with your collaborator often to keep a positive relationship.
- Set clear goals so you can measure success.

In case you're wondering how to find and contact potential collaborators, the recently launched Shopify Collabs is a great place to start.

PRO HACK

Timeliness is key. Let's say you're at an event and you run into one of your industry's top influencers. Jump on the opportunity and stage a quick video interview. You just got some great video content to share with your network.

DAY 15: COLLABORATING WITH BRANDS

Brands in your niche can be a consistent source of work. Retailers often need freelancers to fill gaps when they can't retain skilled marketers. And overworked influencers might also turn to you for extra support. So, building connections here benefits everyone.

HOW BRANDS CHOOSE WHO TO COLLABORATE WITH

- You need to have a strong reputation and a loyal following.
- Your audience must match the brand's target demographic.
- Your content style and values should align with the brand's message.

BENEFITS OF COLLABORATION

- You as an influencer have built trust with your viewers. That means your product endorsements feel more credible than common adverts.
- Influencer product demos also tend to drive more sales.
- Live events usually see high viewer engagement.
- For you, collaborations with brands not only give you more content ideas but also boost your earnings through sponsorships.

TIPS FOR SUCCESSFUL COLLABORATION

- Before you do any work for or with a brand, create a formal contract outlining the terms of the collaboration, including usage rights, payment details and content guidelines.

Platforms like Collabstr, Afluencer, GRIN and Aspire make it easy for you and retailers to find each other and foster partnerships.

SCALING YOUR OPERATIONS
DAY 15: IN-PERSON & ONLINE
INTERVIEWS

Live interviews are exciting because they're full of surprises and unique moments. As a host, you get to meet fascinating guests and share engaging stories, while your viewers get an authentic, real-time experience. They're a great way to connect, spark conversations and keep things fresh for everyone involved.

As host, you'll have to juggle a few things, all while actively listening and responding to your guest. To help it all go smoothly, here are eight easy-to-follow tips for running live interviews.

Before the Interview

KNOW YOUR GUEST

Don't skip this step. It can lead to awkward moments for you, your guest and the audience. Take the time to learn all you can about them. Watch past interviews they've done to come up with fresh questions that make your interview unique.

PLAN AN APPROACH

Think about what your viewers want and match it with your guest's expertise. For example, if they're the founder of a smart activewear brand, focus on the tech for a tech audience or workout benefits for fitness fans. With a clear focus, you can start to write down what you're going to ask your guest.

PLAN THE ACTION

Think about how you want to shoot the interview, keeping your budget and resources in mind. Decide on angles, cuts, the set and background that suit your vision. Watch other interviews on TV or online for inspiration. Pay attention to transitions, cuts and viewpoints, then adapt those ideas to fit your style and possibilities.

For online interviews, plan how you'll transition between speakers, manage screen sharing or spotlight the guest.

INFORM YOUR GUEST

Let your guest know about the interview plan, unless they like spontaneity. Share the topics and provide an outline to help them prepare, ease their nerves and ensure a smooth conversation. It also helps you build a relationship with your guest, which is key to a great interview.

During the Interview

INTRODUCTION

Prepare a short intro of your guest and their achievements or ask if they'd prefer to introduce themselves.

FOCUS ON YOUR GUEST

Stay focused on your guest. Many hosts struggle to listen closely while planning the next question and end up repeating what's already been answered.

ASK GOOD QUESTIONS

Good questions equal cool answers. Go for "How," "Why" and "What" instead of yes-or-no, and plan some follow-ups to keep it interesting.

LET VIEWERS ASK QUESTIONS

Viewers love to feel part of the action. Ask for their questions, pick the best ones and give them a shoutout by name. Offer to circle back after the stream to engage further.

DAY 16: STREAMLINE YOUR DAY, SUPERCHARGE YOUR OUTPUT

Ever wonder how the highest earning live sellers make it look so easy? Their secret lies in creating smart workflows and automating repetitive tasks to free themselves to focus on what truly matters: having fun engaging with their audience and closing deals.

Here's a list of ways you can do it too and how much time it could save you.

TASK	ACTION	TIME SAVED
Replying to support emails	Writing out email replies wastes a lot of time. Instead, develop a library of canned responses for common questions about product details, shipping, returns, etc.	Estimated time saving: 1-2 hours/week
Sending order emails	Set up automated emails to confirm order placement and to provide updates.	Estimated time saving: 15 minutes/order
Sending shipping emails	Set up automated emails with tracking information when an order ships.	Estimated time saving: 15 minutes/order

QUICK TIP
Don't try to automate everything at once. Start with the tasks that take up the most time or cause the most frustration, then gradually expand your automation efforts.

QUICK TIP
There are tools out there, like RescueTime, that identify how you spend your time. You might be surprised! With this data, you can see which daily tasks could be streamlined.

TASK	ACTION	TIME SAVED
Designing visuals	Free tools like Canva and Adobe Express let you quickly create visuals from thousands of pre-made templates.	Estimated time saving: 4 hours/week
Posting on social media	Use a social media management tool to pre-schedule promo posts and announcements of upcoming live events.	Estimated time saving: 1 hour/week
Fulfilling orders	If you're not already, consider using a third-party fulfillment center to handle warehousing, packing and shipping.	Estimated time saving: 15 minutes/order
Daily planning	Keep track of what needs to be done daily/weekly/monthly using a calendar or time management tool.	Estimated time saving: 30 minutes/day

Some tools let you delegate tasks and get notified on updates; perfect if you have a VA (see next page).

DAY 16: HIRE AND TRAIN A VIRTUAL ASSISTANT

You'll be well aware by now just how many tasks are involved in prepping and hosting a successful live selling event. To make things easier, get someone to help you.

Where to Find Virtual Assistants

A virtual assistant (VA) is a freelancer who works remotely and performs various admin-y tasks for you so you can reclaim your time for core business tasks.

Common tasks your VA can help you with include:

- in-stream support (video switching, comment moderation, calendar management)
- customer support (in-app & email)
- order fulfillment
- social media management
- data entry

To hire a VA for live selling, you can use freelancer marketplaces like Upwork, Fiverr, Guru and Freelancer. Or reach out to VA services that specialize in:

- ecommerce in your country
- ecommerce on your chosen platform (e.g., Amazon)
- social media management
- content creation
- customer service
- marketing

Each freelancer marketplace has a wide range of virtual assistants, and you can filter by cost, skills, experience and location.

Having such a wide pool of talent to choose from is a double-edged sword. Knowing what to look for in a VA helps.

What to Look for in a VA

It's possible you'll only interact with your VA in writing, so you want them to have good writing skills and be quick to respond to you. And if you want them to moderate comments on your live stream and/or provide customer support, then strong communication skills becomes even more important.

They should be tech-savvy, with some experience with the platform and tools you use. You want someone who can manage their own time and handle their day-to-day tasks independently. If you find yourself needing to micromanage your VA, you might as well do their tasks yourself.

That said, there will be a period at the start where you'll need to mentor your VA and find your "groove" for working together.

How to Hire and Train a VA

Finding and training a virtual assistant can feel like a big task but breaking it down into simple steps makes it much easier!

Once you've figured out what tasks to outsource and your budget, then pick candidates who match your needs. Choose your favorite, but chat with them first to ensure they're the right fit!

- Check out popular freelancer marketplaces to see which one offers the most suitable candidates for your needs.
- Jot down the tasks you'd like the VA to take off your plate. This'll help you filter the list of potential VAs on your chosen marketplace.
- Decide how much you can spend, whether it's per hour or project.
- Make a shortlist of potential VAs, check their reviews and reach out to them for an initial chat.
- Hire a VA and ease them into their role step by step, making sure they know what's expected and how to get things done.
- Keep an eye on their progress and share your thoughts to help them stay on track.

DAY 16: INTEGRATING LIVE INTO YOUR MARKETING ECOSYSTEM SEAMLESSLY

Live selling is brilliant. But putting all your eggs in one basket means you lose the ability to adapt to changing trends.

That's why live selling works even better when it's part of a broader strategy. Diversifying with other digital tools like social media and email gives you more reach and resilience.

For example, imagine you toiled for months building a thriving brand as a live seller on Facebook. Everything seems to be running smoothly until Facebook unexpectedly announces that it's discontinuing its live shopping feature (yes, it actually happened). Now you're scrambling to adapt. Can your business survive when your viewers feel less connected to you? Can you sell products when you can't demonstrate them or answer questions about them in real time?

This scenario highlights the importance of diversification. If you had integrated live selling into your broader digital sales strategy, then you'd be better equipped to pivot. In other words, you're never entirely reliant on one tool or channel. If one part of your digital ecosystem has a sudden disruption, your brand is protected.

Dedicate time to posting on multiple social media platforms, building out your website and maintaining an email list. This ensures you maintain a consistent presence and connection with your viewers. And if that scenario above were to happen to you, you'd still be making sales, giving you more time to establish a presence on a different live selling platform.

PRIORITIZING YOUR DIGITAL ECOSYSTEM

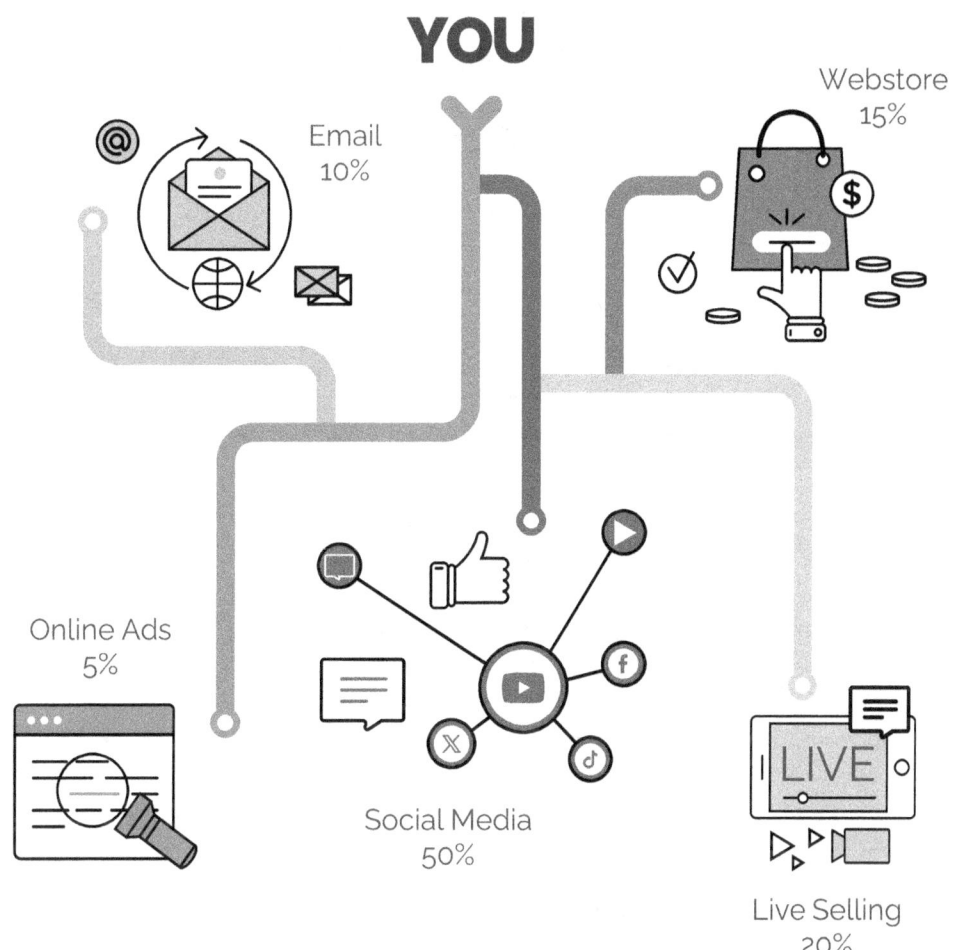

PRO HACK
Record your live sessions and then edit them into shorts you can reuse across your channels.

Pour most of your time into social media, creating a constant flow of engaging posts. It's your primary stage for building brand awareness and connections with viewers. Your live events complement your social efforts, while a strong email marketing strategy and keeping your web store fresh help to support your online sales.

DAY 16: A VERY BRIEF GUIDE TO EMAIL MARKETING

Email marketing is a great way to stay connected with your viewers with friendly reminders about upcoming live events or new arrivals and special promotions in your store.

Entire books have been written about email marketing. Tbh that's true of many subjects in this book. But I'll try and give a high-level overview of an effective email strategy you can look more into.

Build Your Subscriber List

Growing your email list is the first step. Use your live streams to invite viewers to subscribe. The usual practice is to offer something special like a discount, an exclusive video, or early-bird access to a new product.

- **DO** keep the sign-up process simple, with a catchy call-to-action and a visible link to a form.
- **DON'T** buy an email list. It's a bad investment. These lists have low-quality leads, not to mention compliance issues.

QUICK TIP

Many email marketing tools like Mailchimp offer free trials or basic plans. They have limited features but are perfect for testing while your email list is still small before committing to an expensive plan.

Craft Emails that Speak to Your Audience

Your emails should always hold value to your viewers. But you'll still need attention-grabbing subject lines that make viewers excited to open. Think "Tune In Tonight for VIP Access to the Next Live Sale!" and a link or calendar invite to your live stream so they can jump straight in.

Keep your content clear and visually appealing with short text and a tone that feels relatable and friendly. Your emails should always make your viewers feel like you're speaking directly to them.

- **DO** keep emails focused on a single topic or outcome you're aiming for.
- **DON'T** spam your viewers. If you email too often, they'll opt out.

Make Data Work for You

Keep an eye on how your emails perform. Track metrics like open rates and click-through rates to learn what works best for your viewers. And if they aren't engaging with promotional emails, try tweaking the content.

- **DO** segment your list based on interests, time zone, buying habits, etc. and look for ways to personalize emails as much as possible.
- **DON'T** send the exact same email to all your viewers at the same time.

Stay Consistent

You've heard it a million times already (sorry), but consistency really is key to keeping your audience engaged. Establish a regular schedule for your emails, maybe once a week or tied to your live event dates. Always stay true to your brand identity, using the same style, tone and visuals in every email so your viewers feel familiar with your content.

- **DO** encourage feedback. You've got a community, ask them what they want.
- **DON'T** let email marketing dominate your time and energy. Focus on having fun with your live events.

YOU TOTALLY GOT THIS

Stellar growth! Ready to amplify your success?

DAY 14:

❑ Design an A/B experiment to refine your approach.

❑ Introduce new products based on demand.

❑ Learn cross-selling and upselling techniques.

DAY 15:

❑ Think about valuable giveaways for your viewers.

❑ Learn about effective loyalty programs.

❑ Consider reaching out and collaborating with others.

DAY 16:

❑ Streamline your processes to save you time.

❑ Look into hiring a virtual assistant.

❑ Define where live selling fits into your business.

PERFECTING YOUR CRAFT

DAY 17: THE MAGIC OF
BEING REAL

Trust isn't just a buzzword, it's a critical part of successful selling.

This is how it goes: Your viewers are more likely to buy from you when they believe you're honest and reliable. That trust makes viewers more interactive, asking questions and sharing feedback. And more interaction turns one-time buyers into repeat customers.

But how do you go about making viewers trust you?

SHARE WHAT MAKES YOU DIFFERENT

Stories are powerful tools for connection. Your personal story is your unique selling point. Try sharing how you discovered the product, how it fits into your life and how it solves problems you've faced.

BE GENUINE AND TRANSPARENT

Your authenticity begins with honesty. Share your true thoughts and feelings about the products you showcase. And while preparing a script before you go live is key, try not to sound rehearsed or else it can come off as insincere.

BEHIND-THE-SCENES CONTENT

Give a glimpse of where you work or create and show how your products are made or prepared. Letting your audience see the real you and introducing the people who help you adds a human touch.

CELEBRATE IMPERFECTION

Perfection isn't relatable, being human is. If something goes wrong during a live event, own it. You could even use it to sprinkle in some humor.

BE ACCESSIBLE

Let viewers know how they can reach you outside of livestreams. Make a real effort to reply promptly to messages and comments on other platforms and keep the conversation going.

STAY TRUE TO YOU AND YOUR VALUES

Let your principles guide your interactions. That way, you'll steer clear of behaviors that erode trust like lying, being too pushy with sales, and badmouthing other sellers.

MAKE INTERACTION A TWO-WAY STREET

Show that you value your viewers' input. One way you can do that is by acknowledging viewers by name and answering their questions. Practice active listening and adapt your stream based on feedback, showing that you take their input seriously.

EMMA THE AUTHENTIC COOK

Imagine Emma, a home chef who sells kitchen gadgets through her livestreams.

She shares both her culinary triumphs and disasters, making her relatable. (authentic)

Viewers see her unedited cooking process, including the messes. (behind the scenes)

Emma hosts weekly cook-alongs, encouraging viewers to participate in real-time. (community)

She's upfront about shipping times and potential delays. (transparent)

Her honesty and openness have built a loyal following that trusts her advice and looks forward to her streams.

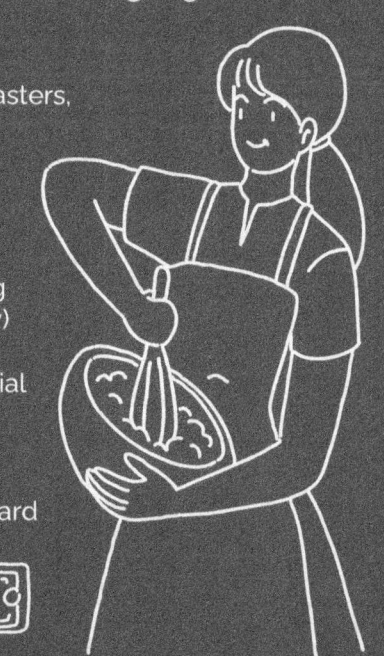

DAY 17: GRABBING ATTENTION LIKE A PRO

It's not enough to simply showcase a product, you need to captivate your audience, spark their curiosity and inspire them to take action. The AIDA model is your secret weapon. It's the art that transforms a standard sales pitch into a memorable experience. Here's how you can use AIDA, **Attention, Interest, Desire, Action**, in your product showcases.

KEEP THE INTEREST ALIVE

Once you've got their attention, it's time to reel them in deeper. Share a relatable experience, like if you're selling a skincare product, you could say, "I used to dread mornings until I discovered this product." And then show real-time results by applying it live and letting viewers see the transformation. Ask for Input: "What makes you dread the morning skincare routine? Drop it in the chat!"

BOLD OPENINGS THAT HOOK

First things first: you need to stop viewers in their tracks. Kick off with something that makes your audience think. "What if you could transform your style with just one accessory?" Or hit them with a surprising statement like, "I've been doing it wrong all along, and so have you." You could even use eye-catching imagery or unexpected props to draw eyes and make viewers stick around.

PRO HACK

Viewers get bored if things stay the same for too long. To keep them engaged, play around with camera angles and other video sources. This is what good news broadcasts do with their multiple viewpoints and added visuals.

INSPIRE IMMEDIATE ACTION

You've stoked the desire; now channel it into action. Make your call to action direct, clear and compelling. How? Make it sound simple by walking them through the purchase steps. "Just tap the link, choose your color, and you're all set." Sprinkle in some scarcity tactics to create a sense of FOMO like, "Only 5 left in stock, these are flying off the shelves!" Use it sparingly though.

D

A

BUILD AN IRRESISTIBLE DESIRE

Interest piques curiosity, but desire compels action. It's a bit of a mouthful but it's true. If you focus on benefits not features, you can paint a picture in their minds. Try, "Imagine breezing through your tasks and having extra time for what you love, all because of this organizer." Or appeal to their emotions with something like, "Feel confident and unstoppable every time you wear this."

DAY 17: HOW TO HANDLE OBJECTIONS

Every viewer is a potential customer and advocate for your brand. By addressing their concerns thoughtfully, you show you value them beyond just a sale. Expect many of the same objections from viewers. But beware because they usually don't directly voice them. It's up to you to see subtle clues and read between the lines to turn doubts and hesitations into sales.

What most of your viewers are thinking

VALUE FOR MONEY
Does the price justify the benefits?

RELEVANCE
Does the product fit my specific needs or lifestyle?

CREDIBILITY
Do I trust you?

Before you can address these unspoken concerns, you need to recognize the subtle signals that indicate a viewer's hesitations.

Clues in Viewer Behavior and Comments

COMMENT FREQUENCY
A sudden drop in comments might indicate people are confused or are losing interest.

REPEATED THEMES
Multiple questions about the same topic suggest lingering doubts you haven't addressed yet or enough.

EMOJIS AND REACTIONS
A string of skeptical emojis can signal doubt or disbelief about whether the product truly works as you say it does.

You can ease your viewers' minds by addressing their worries early on. Even better if you can do it before they even think of them. As you do more and more livestreams and gain experience, you'll be able to handle these like a pro. For now, here are some ideas on how to handle the most common objections.

Response strategies for silent objections

I THINK IT'S TOO EXPENSIVE
Explain what goes into the price like quality materials, innovative technology, etc. and even make a comparison: "Unlike other brands that cost twice as much, this one includes lifetime updates." You can also highlight your product's long-term value: "While it's an investment, just think how much you'll save over time by not having to buy refills."

I'M NOT SURE IT'S FOR ME
Viewers don't yet see how relevant the product is to them and their lifestyle. Address it with a user testimonial: "Alex from New York was skeptical at first but now swears by it for his daily routine."

Your product demos must also show the products versatility: "This product is designed to adapt to various needs, whether you're a professional or a beginner. Let me show you how easy it is to customize settings for your specific preferences."

I CAN FIND A SIMILAR PRODUCT ELSEWHERE
This is where you have to really think about how the unique features of your product translate into unique benefits. It can be a product feature: "This model includes an exclusive feature that simplifies your daily tasks, making life easier for you." Or say something about aftersales support: "It comes with a two-year warranty, double the industry standard, giving you peace of mind and saving you from potential repair costs."

I NEED TO THINK ABOUT IT
This is where your old friend urgency comes in. But don't pressure anyone. Try: "Just so you know, this special offer is available until midnight." If available, you can offer extra resources: "I'll send a brochure with more details to help you make an informed decision."

162 | PERFECTING YOUR CRAFT
DAY 18: SCARCITY TACTICS. AKA
FOMO

FOMO is the Fear of Missing Out. It taps into our deep-rooted need to belong and seize exciting opportunities. It's mostly fueled by social media and most of the emotions people associate with FOMO are negative, like envy and sadness.

But used wisely and ethically, FOMO can motivate people to take positive action. And in the realm of live selling, it can be a powerful driver for boosting sales and engagement.

Here's a crazy statistic as reported by OptinMonster in 2025:

60% of millennials make a purchase because of **FOMO**

For anyone not familiar with the term, Millennials (also known as Generation Y, or Gen Y) are people born between 1981 and 1996, and as of 2025, they are between the ages of 28 and 43. It's an age group you'll likely attract to your streams.

Using FOMO effectively means creating a sense of urgency and exclusivity around your products. When your viewers find out there's limited availability of a product, especially one that already has positive reviews, it increases the perceived value of your product. And this scarcity (and social proof as a booster) is what drives viewers to want to buy the product too.

Here are three ways to use FOMO effectively:

LIMITED TIME OFFERS

When you time-bound an offer, it creates a sense of urgency that encourages viewers to take action before it's too late. Here's an example: *"For the next 15 minutes, get 20% off and free shipping on all orders!"*

You'll learn more about limited time offers on the next pages.

EXCLUSIVE PRODUCTS

Unique products like special edition items and bundles that provide extra value create a sense of exclusivity. Combine these with limited availability and it makes the offer even more irresistible. An example could be: *"Get this exclusive bundle, available only during today's livestream!"*

LIMITED PRODUCT QUANTITY

For when you genuinely don't have a large quantity left of a popular product or a free gift. It encourages viewers to act early or miss out. You could say: *"The first 20 buyers will receive an extra gift with their purchase!"*

Some good tactics include pre-order discounts and VIP access.

BE HONEST AND TRANSPARENT

Always be truthful about the availability of your products and that your limited-time or limited-quantity offers are legitimate. And don't use any pressure tactics. Aim to balance urgency with respect for your viewer's decision-making process.

DAY 18: LIMITED-TIME OFFERS & FLASH SALES

Something that a lot of live streamers often forget, especially when starting out, is that the audience needs to be constantly motivated. This is true of any media, from print publications to TV. One of the best tactics to have in your arsenal as a live seller is a limited-time offer.

A limited-time offer is, for example, telling your viewers that certain products will be discounted for the next X number of minutes or that you'll be giving something for free to the first Y number of people that make a purchase. Because these offers don't last very long, they're also known as flash sales.

And that's the point. When people see they only have a short window to snag a great deal, they're more likely to act quickly. It's not that you're pressuring anyone to buy something they don't want. In fact, the special offer feels unique and exclusive, and by taking advantage of it, your viewers put more value on the products they're buying. That means they're happier with their purchase from you and more likely to buy from you again and leave a positive review.

PRO HACK

Limited-time offers and flash sales are great for clearing excess stock, especially if you sell seasonal products. Shoppers are eager to get a good deal before the end of the season and you get to free up valuable storage space for new products.

THE BEST FLASH SALES HAVE

- Attention-grabbing graphics
- A compelling offer
- A clear time frame
- Exclusivity

9 IRRESISTIBLE FLASH SALE IDEAS

Run exclusive flash deals during the holidays so your viewers know they can't hang around if they want to save.

Add a live countdown timer that shows shoppers exactly how many seconds remain to grab your flash sale offers. Turn the page to learn more.

Sweeten the deal by offering free delivery or a complimentary gift that's only available to shoppers during the limited-time event.

Encourage positive reviews by offering exclusive, time-bound discount codes as a thank-you bonus.

Entice first-time buyers with a special discount that's only available for a brief window.

Craft custom, short-term discounts based on each viewer's previous purchases, making them feel individually valued.

Use exit-intent popups to deliver a last-second, time-sensitive discount that catches potential buyers before they leave.

Surprise viewers at checkout with mystery discounts that appear with a ticking timer, urging them to complete their purchase fast.

Send post-purchase emails that hint at upcoming time-limited deals, keeping your viewers excited for the next opportunity.

DAY 18: ADDING COUNTDOWN TIMERS TO YOUR LIVESTREAM

Adding a countdown timer is a smart move. It lets you share the stream with your audience before going live, which gives you time to prepare while building excitement. The countdown timer makes viewers want to stay and see what happens when the timer is over. Plus, it adds a professional and organized touch to your broadcast, making it look polished and inviting.

Countdown timers have many other great uses too. You can show when a sale ends during a live stream. They're also perfect for new product releases and giveaways, keeping your audience engaged as they wait for the big moment.

And it isn't limited to timers. You could show product quantity in real time, so that when a viewer buys, the quantity goes down. Amazon and Etsy listings are great examples of this.

WHAT MAKES A GOOD COUNTDOWN TIMER

EASY TO MAKE

Creating a countdown timer should be super simple with no tech skills required. There's a bunch of tools out there that can build these.

EASY TO USE

It should have a user-friendly design you can easily set and forget or start it with a single click. You need to focus on the event, not the timer.

BRANDABLE

Make sure you can make the timer uniquely yours like adding your photo and your brand's colors and logo for a cohesive, professional look.

EFFECTIVE COUNTDOWN TIMER EXAMPLES

Branded show countdown

Collect email addresses

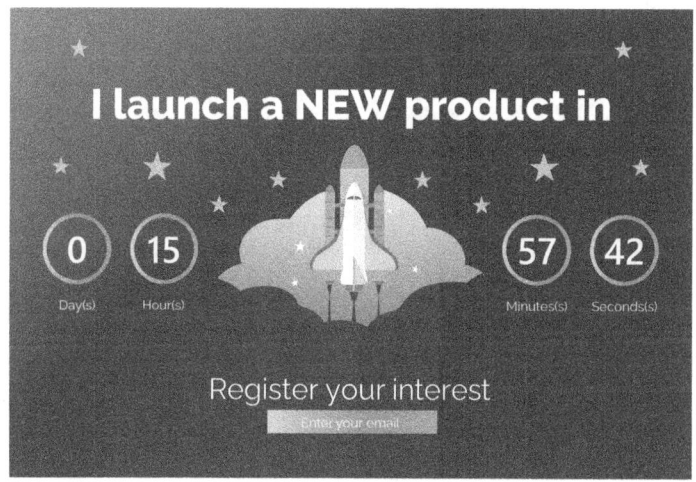

In-stream offers

DAY 19: LEVERAGING SOCIAL PROOF

QUICK TIP
What you say about your products is important, but it matters much less than what others say about them (and about you). That's why social proof is so important in live selling.

The average customer reads 10 online reviews before they but something. It's because they're on the fence and aren't sure if they should hit the Buy button or not. And rather than trust their own intuition, they look for what other people are doing before deciding what to do.

It's called *social proof*. It's a powerful marketing tool because it leverages our human desire to fit in, influencing what we choose to buy. In case you're curious about the psychology behind social proof, it taps into these three powerful principles:

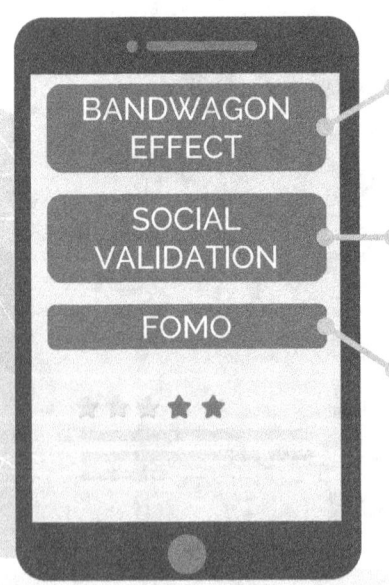

BANDWAGON EFFECT — People tend to mirror the actions of others, like noticing a notification that someone has purchased the same product.

SOCIAL VALIDATION — Seeing others interact with a product reassures potential buyers and strengthens their confidence in making a choice.

FOMO — You learned about Fear Of Missing Out yesterday. It's when updates on limited stock or high demand prompt quicker decisions to avoid missing out on an opportunity.

These psychological triggers can shape how your viewers decide to buy during your live events. By using them wisely, you can boost sales and help your audience feel good about their choices.

HOW SOCIAL PROOF BENEFITS YOU

Social proof is clearly an awesome way to build trust and boost your sales. And it's driven directly by satisfied viewers. That makes it authentic. It can come in the form of things like customer testimonials, case studies, reviews and endorsements (you'll learn how to gather and manage social proof on the next pages).

Real testimonials show that you can actually deliver on your promises. So, even if you're hyping your products as the best things since sliced bread, nothing beats a genuine thumbs-up from someone who confirms that they're the real deal. And that goes for trusting you as the seller too.

When your viewers see real stories and honest feedback, it washes away any doubts they have about making the choice to buy. You want your viewers to feel confident about their decision because they'll be more satisfied with their purchase, and that means they're more likely to leave a positive review themselves. Roughly 20% of consumers write reviews, so it's definitely worth leveraging social proof as it helps you build a trustworthy reputation and turns curious viewers into loyal customers.

DAY 19: LEVERAGING SOCIAL PROOF:
CRUSH IT IN STREAMS

Learn how to effectively gather, present and leverage social proof to enhance your live events and build trust with viewers in real time.

WAYS TO GET THE MOST OUT OF SOCIAL PROOF WHEN YOU'RE LIVE

COMMENTS

Real-time comments build social proof because they show potential buyers that other viewers are hyped about the product, leaving comments and asking questions. When viewers see excitement from others, they feel reassured and less hesitant to hit the Buy button.

TIP: Pin or read out the best comments.

POPUP NOTIFICATIONS

Imagine viewers are watching you live. Suddenly, a message appears, saying someone has snagged one of your products. They won't help but feel the urge to join them before they're gone. If your platform allows it, show who bought the product, where they're from, what they bought and when they bought it. This info makes the alert legit. Make the product image clickable or add a button that links to the product for viewers to also buy it.

Show who's buying and reviewing.

Show comments and reactions.

VIDEOS

Play videos from real clients during your live selling events. Video testimonials are a powerful way to tap into social proof and drive sales because they're a visual "proof" that the product delivers what it promises, making new viewers feel more confident about buying.

TIP: Aim for bite-sized clips that quickly highlight key benefits.

172 | PERFECTING YOUR CRAFT

DAY 19: LEVERAGING SOCIAL PROOF:
CRUSH IT ELSEWHERE

Learn how to effectively gather, present and leverage social proof to build trust with viewers as part of your overall marketing strategy.

WAYS TO GET THE MOST OUT OF SOCIAL PROOF WHEN YOU'RE NOT LIVE

TESTIMONIALS *(from verified buyers)*

Testimonials are different from reviews. They're usually a bit more in-depth and focused on positive experiences. Basically, it's an endorsement from a satisfied customer. Pop these on your website (if you have one), your social channels, visuals, sign-up forms, emails and ads.

Alex Jones

Every time I tune into Fern's live session, I feel like I'm hanging out with a friend who's just being real. Her authenticity shines through. No sugarcoating, just honest advice that actually helps me decide. It's refreshing to see someone put it all out there, and that's why I keep coming back.

TIP: Showing the name (and photo, if you can and have permission) of who left the testimonial proves to others that it's authentic.

REVIEWS

Reviews are usually short and include a rating out of five stars. They can include what your viewer liked and things they weren't such a huge a fan of. Your product pages can list all reviews, while you can share the positive ones in your social posts.

Include info like a "Verified Buyer" label and the date to prove they're genuine.

Another cool feature that taps in social proof is displaying the combined rating and an AI-written summary of reviews. A tagline like "100% of buyers recommend the product" encourages others to purchase confidently.

POPUP NOTIFICATIONS

There are a bunch of free and paid tools that can help you add real-time notifications like user activity, customer feedback and other trust signals on your website. For example, if a viewer lands on your site and sees a popup with a new review or that "Pat from Seattle just bought this," it creates a sense of activity and trust.

OTHER TRUST SIGNALS

- TRUSTED BY: Show logos of brands you work with.
- AS FEATURED IN: Logos of any media you were mentioned in.
- STATS: If you have a large following, show it in numbers.
- AWARDS: Highlight any recognition and awards.
- PROFESSIONAL ENDORSEMENT AND AFFILIATIONS

174 | PERFECTING YOUR CRAFT

DAY 20: IDENTIFYING YOUR BEST TIMES TO STREAM

Streaming when your audience is available means more viewers.

Viewers are more likely to interact when they are actively watching.

Higher viewership and engagement leads to more sales.

You've got some options when it comes to figuring out your best times to go live. Some you can do now, others you'll do routinely. But they're all super simple, so I recommend you do all of them.

WHAT YOU CAN DO NOW

COMPETITORS	TARGET AUDIENCE

Look for others who sell the same products as you or products aimed at the same audience as you. Jot down the times they sell and what kind of viewing figures they get. Try out these times for yourself and see what kind of results you get.	Think about who your viewers are and when they're online. Like if you sell kid's clothing, avoid going live after 10pm when many parents are already asleep. And while 8pm suits people in your time zone, viewers elsewhere might still be at work.

WHAT YOU CAN DO ROUTINELY

TESTING

Go live on different days and at different times to find your audience's sweet spot. You could try streaming on weekday evenings and weekend mornings and then compare viewership and engagement.

They'll be some trial and error with this one, so be willing to adapt your streaming times based on changing trends and audience behavior. You might even notice a trend towards an irregular time, like having more lunchtime viewers, so think about adding midday streams to your schedule.

ANALYSIS

Keep track of your results. That means keeping a record of viewer numbers, engagement and sales for each day and time. Look for consistent patterns in the data to identify the best times. For data analysis, use a simple spreadsheet and filter the data, or see if your platform can provide useful metrics.

Another good way to gather data on the best streaming times for your viewers is to simply ask them. Ask during your livestreams for their preferred times. A simple poll works well for this.

YOUR BEST TIMES MUST SUIT YOU TOO!

It's all very well finding the best times to do your live events, but it must work for your schedule too! Like if you have young children at home, you might need to go live after they've gone to bed because it's just not feasible at any other time. If that's the case for you, try figuring out the best streaming time within a specific range, say 8pm to 11pm.

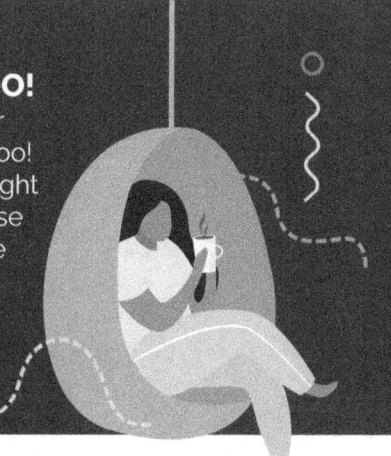

DAY 20: PLANNING A
THEME FOR A STREAM

When it comes to live selling, viewers tend to be more influenced by educational content. That means they're more likely to buy if you do a good job describing product features and benefits than if you just shared colorful visuals and be more entertaining.

But that doesn't mean you can't have a little fun with it. And with themed events, you can create a sense of anticipation and excitement before the event as well as make your live events more memorable and shareable.

STEP 1: CHOOSE A RELEVANT THEME
I say relevant because your chosen theme should resonate with your audience and align with your brand.

- **Seasonal**: See the next pages for more about celebrating holidays and seasonal events.
- **Carnival**: Create a "Rio Carnival" themed event with samba music and vibrant costumes.
  - **Coachella**: Recreate the festival vibe featuring music, fashion and art.
    - **Decades**: Take your viewers on a nostalgic journey with a themed event from a specific decade.
    - **Sports**: Engage sports fans with a themed stream centered around a big sporting event.
    - **Food and Drink**: Delight foodies with a themed event focused on culinary experiences.

STEP 2: PLAN FUN ACTIVITIES

Incorporate interactive activities that align with your theme to keep viewers engaged. For example, let's say you wanna host a 90s music event. You could run a 90s music trivia quiz and a costume contest, with prizes for the best dressed and quiz winner. Just be aware that viewers tend to engage more with activities that require less involvement and when they don't have to be on camera.

STEP 3: CREATE VISUALS AND PROMOTE

Make themed graphics and overlays that you'll use in your livestream. Keep it simple here cos you don't wanna detract from the main purpose of your stream. All graphics should align with your branding that you developed on Day 5.

Promote the event across multiple channels well in advance to avoid a low turnout. Build anticipation and excitement for your event, like making a cool landing page, blasting your email list, hyping it on socials, dropping it on your blog, and if you can, boosting it with some ads.

STEP 4: DRESS TO IMPRESS AND ENGAGE

Before you go live, set up themed decorations in your livestream space. Dress up in a costume that matches your theme. Imagine if you're doing a "Summer Beach Party" theme, then decorate your space with beach balls, palm trees and tropical flowers and wear a Hawaiian shirt and sunglasses. Ask viewers to drop a comment in the chat with their favorite summer anthems that you can play in the background.

DAY 20: MAXIMIZING SALES IN THE SEASONS

Your viewers' buying behavior changes throughout the year. In summer, for example, people spend their money on things they can use outdoors and on their travels. It's also a time when people work on their houses and gardens, and towards the end, parents are getting ready for their kids going back to school. When winter rolls around, people start looking for things to keep them warm. They're also looking for gifts and seasonal discounts.

SEASONAL TRENDS AND HOLIDAYS

- SPRING CLEANING
- MOTHER'S DAY
- GARDENING
- EASTER
- INDOORS
- CHRISTMAS
- WARM GEAR
- VALENTINE'S DAY
- COOL GEAR
- FATHER'S DAY
- OUTDOORS
- TRAVEL
- HALLOWEEN
- THANKSGIVING
- BACK TO SCHOOL
- BLACK FRIDAY

GO LIVE & THRIVE - DAY 20 | **179**

Different times of the year bring unique opportunities and challenges that can impact your sales. By predicting the buying behavior of your viewers in an upcoming season, you can plan and adjust your sales strategies based on the time of year. If you do it right, Black Friday won't be the only day of the year where buyers turn into professional wrestlers and battle for the best deals.

3-6 MONTHS BEFORE

Planning Phase
Identify the seasonal trend or event. Pick out key products that'll resonate during that time. If it's something new, start the design process so they're ready for launch.

2-3 MONTHS BEFORE

Prep Phase
Start developing marketing content for the seasonal theme, like visuals, videos and text. You'll also wanna confirm inventory levels. Order extra stock if necessary

1 MONTH BEFORE

Pre-Promo Phase
Begin creating buzz with teaser posts, sneak peeks or countdowns on social media and other channels. Start to plan your livestream events.

2-4 WEEKS BEFORE

Kick off Phase
Officially launch your seasonal marketing campaign across all platforms. Introduce the seasonal-themed products and time-limited deals you'll be offering.

1 WEEK BEFORE

Engagement Phase
Increase the frequency of your posts. Make use of stories, reels and live updates to stay top-of-mind. Be highly responsive to comments and messages.

IMMEDIATELY AFTER

Follow-Up Phase
Send thank-you messages to buyers. Check your analytics to see how your seasonal campaign went. What can you improve for the next event?

QUICK TIP

Take advantage of industry-specific events and trends that can happen at any time of year. It depends on your products, but it could be things like fashion events, tech conventions and health and wellness months.

Btw, selling based on seasonal trends and events is totally optional. If what you're doing with your regular streams and products is working, then stick with that.

YOU TOTALLY GOT THIS

Smashed it! Time to reap the rewards!

DAY 17:

❏ Learn how to be more authentic.

❏ Use AIDA to grab your viewers' attention.

❏ Learn how to deal with objections like a pro.

DAY 18:

❏ Make FOMO part of your sales tactics.

❏ Create limited offers and flash sales.

❏ Design a countdown timer for your next event.

DAY 19:

❏ Learn the benefits of using social proof.

❏ Add social proof to your live events.

❏ Add social proof to your webshop and social channels.

DAY 20:

- ❏ Find the best time of day for your live events.
- ❏ Plan a fun theme for a future event.
- ❏ Learn how to boost sales in each season.

LIGHTS, CAMERA, CHA-CHING!

DAY 21: PRE-EVENT
MARKETING BLITZ

TO YOUR VIEWERS

Ideas to get the word out to your viewers and followers:

- ❏ Share sneak previews about your live event to build excitement.
- ❏ Share teasers about upcoming products (photos & videos) to build curiosity.
- ❏ Launch countdown posts across all of your social platforms.
- ❏ Announce exclusive offers or "early-bird discounts" for those registering or tuning in early.
- ❏ Send engaging emails with event reminders, sneak peeks and exclusive benefits to your subscribers.

WIDER REACH

Ideas to get the word out to reach more potential viewers:

- ❏ Optimize your platforms with event info, banners and polished product pages.
- ❏ Run targeted ads on social media platforms.
- ❏ Post engaging blogs about your event and product lineup on your website.
- ❏ Write a guest blog post about your event and product lineup on someone else's website.
- ❏ Build an event landing page with details, registration links and attractive visuals.

DAY 21: IN-EVENT TACTICS FOR MAXIMIZING SALES

INTERACTION

Ideas to engage and build trust with your viewers:

- ❏ Greet viewers with energy, use their names (when possible) and create a friendly, welcoming atmosphere.
- ❏ Answer viewer questions live.
- ❏ Share quick, positive reviews or user experiences during the stream as social proof.
- ❏ Demo products in action, highlighting key features and benefits while asking for live feedback.
- ❏ Shoutout viewers' comments & purchases to make them feel valued.
- ❏ Run quick contests with prizes to keep energy high.

CALLS TO ACTION

Ideas to drive more sales during and after your event:

- ❏ Pin comments or banners to highlight top offers.
- ❏ Regularly remind viewers to click the Buy button or checkout link, using a mixture of action-oriented phrases like "Grab it before it's gone!"
- ❏ Tap into FOMO to highlight scarcity and promote urgency.
- ❏ Remember to upsell and cross-sell.
- ❏ State your different payment methods or installment plans to remove buying barriers.
- ❏ Before wrapping up, provide a last call for offers to give hesitant buyers one last nudge.

DAY 21: PUTTING ALL THE PIECES TOGETHER
FOR A HIGH-EARNING LIVE EVENT

Look at you:

You know what makes you
and your brand unique

You know the ins and outs
of your chosen platform

You've sourced awesome products
that your viewers will love

You know how to price
your products for profit

You're confident on camera
and know how to keep viewers hooked

You can troubleshoot like a pro

You deliver great customer service to keep viewers happy and loyal

You know how to analyze your performance to spot successes and areas for improvement

You can drive sales with limited-time offers and exclusivity

You know how to leverage viewer feedback to build credibility

You explored strategies for growing your live selling business

You know how to get the word out

You're basically a live selling ninja!

Today is the day when everything you've learned, practiced and perfected comes alive in an earning live selling event.

Go live with calm, confident energy, knowing that you've done the hard work.

188 | LIGHTS, CAMERA, CHA-CHING!

QUICK TIP
Set an earnings target for this event, but don't stress if you don't reach it. Every step is progress, and every sale is a win. Remember to thank your viewers for showing up and supporting you.

DAY 21: YOUR
FIRST SALE$ LIVESTREAM

Go LIVE. Nail it!

YOU TOTALLY GOT THIS

Smashed it! Time to reap the rewards!

DAY 21:

- ❏ Build excitement with content across all channels.

- ❏ Recap what you've learned on your journey.

- ❏ Go live with confidence and have fun!

YOUR Future IS BRIGHT

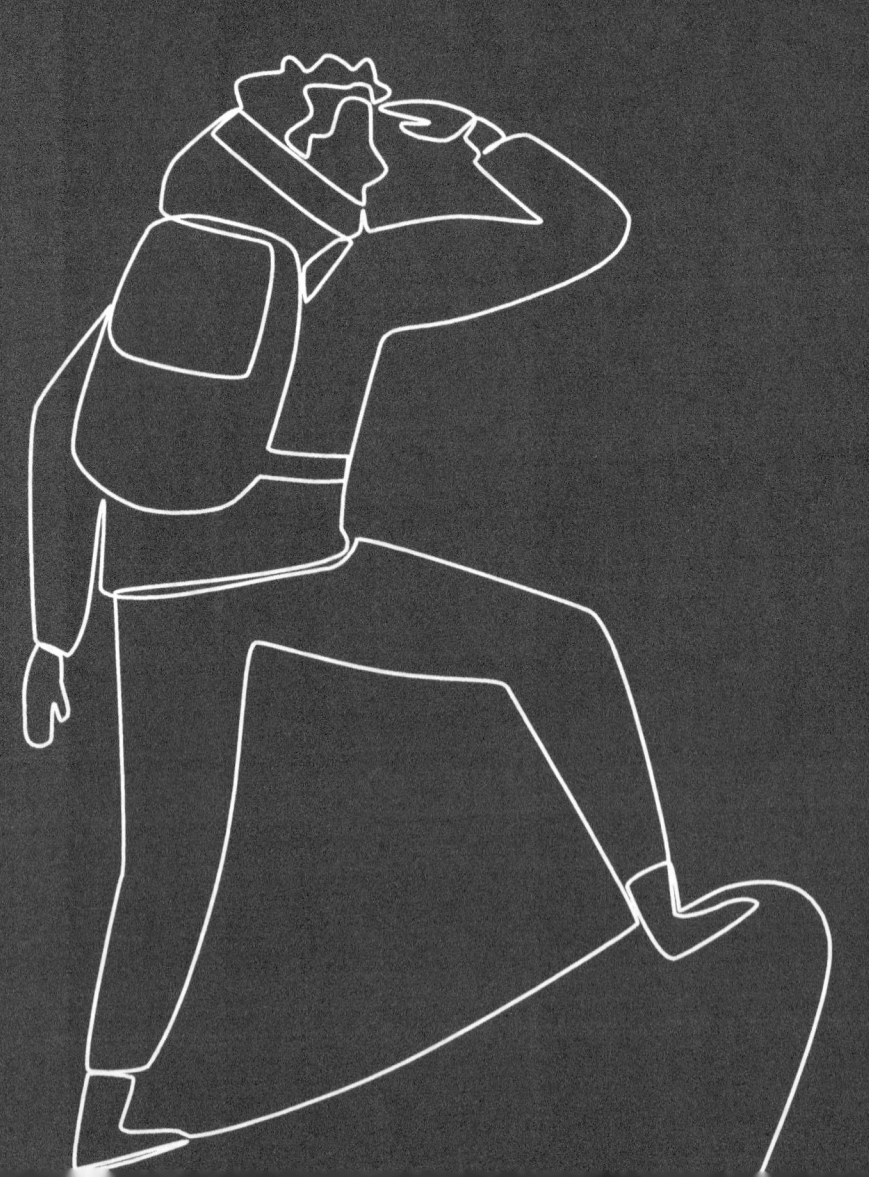

THE ROAD AHEAD

THE ROAD AHEAD

REFLECTING ON YOUR 21-DAY JOURNEY

Taking time to reflect on what you've learned in the past helps you learn critical thinking skills and figure out ways to do even better when facing challenges later on.

Over the last 21 days, you've built a foundation for success as a live seller: building your brand, engaging with viewers and scaling up your operations. Now is the time to unpack it all. What strategies worked particularly well? What didn't quite pan out?

By reviewing your progress and reflecting on your learning, you can sharpen your skills, refine your approach and confidently host live streams with huge audiences.

MAXIMIZE YOUR LEARNING AS A LIVE SELLER

American educational theorist David A. Kolb reckons there are four stages to learning through experience (please don't fall asleep just yet!). By actively engaging with each stage, you'll transform your live selling experiences into powerful learning opportunities. Here's how it applies to your live selling journey:

What happened? Revisit day one. What were your initial expectations? Were you feeling nervous, excited or uncertain? What about that first live stream? Did your technology cooperate? Did you make any sales?

What did you learn? This is the most valuable part. Perhaps you discovered that your viewers respond well to behind-the-scenes content. Or maybe you realized that your initial pricing strategy needed adjustment. Jot down *everything*.

What can you improve? Be honest with yourself. Did you find yourself stumbling over your words? Did you forget to promote your stream in advance? Identify the areas where you know you can perform better.

How will you apply this going forward? This is where you put your insights into action. Turn those lessons into concrete steps. Maybe you improve your pre-stream checklist to ensure proper promotion. Or perhaps you practice your sales pitch to build confidence.

MOMENTS OF DOUBT OFTEN MARK THE START OF SOMETHING GREAT!
If you're feeling anxious or unsure after these 21 days, remind yourself that this is part of growing and improving. Don't let the fear of the unknown stop you. There's advice from an Olympic gold medalist on the next page that can help you take the next step with confidence.

Don't let reflection be a one-off activity. Aim to make it a regular part of your process. Self-reflection in learning offers a unique opportunity to check progress and improve overall understanding.

Schedule 15 minutes each week to review your progress. Ask yourself:
- What am I most proud of accomplishing this week?
- What was the biggest challenge I faced?
- What will be my primary focus next week?

Your 21-day journey marks just the beginning. Live selling is a constantly evolving field. So, continue forward, reflect often and achieve your goals!

196 | THE ROAD AHEAD
WHAT DO YOU DO WHEN YOU WANNA QUIT?
(ADVICE FROM AN OLYMPIC GOLD MEDALIST)

You've prepped an amazing session, but as you go live, hardly anyone turns up, comments are sparse and no-one seems mildly interested in what you're saying or selling. You might say:

> *I hate live selling. It's too hard.*

> *I don't want to do this anymore.*

When the constant hustle of live selling is draining your energy, remember this:

You can quit. But not today.

We all have days when we want to quit. When something feels hard, our brain and body resist because they want us to be comfortable. If you're grappling with this feeling, you're not alone.

Live selling comes with all sorts of challenges that make it feel like you're climbing Mount Everest. Sometimes you'll perform to an almost empty room, sometimes the audio cuts out or your app crashes, sometimes viewers leave harsh comments and reviews and sometimes the rewards just don't match your efforts. Any of these things can make you want to throw in the towel.

But if you quit on a bad day, you'll never become great at live selling, and you might regret it later.

So, here's the deal:

You can quit on a good day.

When you have a successful day and you still want to quit, then you can consider it.

This approach normalizes your struggles and builds resilience. Recognize that tough days are temporary and not a reflection of your overall journey. Feeling the urge to quit is just a natural part of it.

Push through. You're evolving into a stronger, more resilient version of yourself.

This advice was adopted from the words of American Olympic gold medal-winning gymnast Nastia Liukin, whose motto is:

"Never quit on a bad day"

THE ROAD AHEAD

SETTING
NEW GOALS & SCALING UP

Goals are about imagining success. SMART goals are about building a roadmap to get you there. SMART goals are Specific, Measurable, Achievable, Relevant and Time-bound. Put simply, they're a tried-and-true method for turning ideas into action, keeping you focused and moving forward in your live selling career.

Sorry if this is like the gazillionth time in your life that you're hearing about SMART goals, but I'll break it down with live selling in mind:

S

Your goal should be crystal clear. Instead of saying, "I want to do better live streams," aim for something focused like "I want to host live streams twice a week that each generate at least 50 sales." Specific goals provide clarity and direction, helping you stay on track.

M

How will you know you've succeeded? Measuring your progress is key. For example, you might track metrics like viewer engagement, total sales per live stream or average order value. Being able to measure results ensures you can celebrate wins and identify areas for improvement.

THE ROAD AHEAD | 199

QUICK TIP

SMART goals aren't set in stone. They should evolve as you and your business grow. Check your goals regularly to see where you're at. If a goal isn't working or no longer fits your vision, adjust or replace it. And always celebrate wins big and small!

A

Set goals that challenge you but aren't out of reach. You're new to live selling, so start with something realistic, like increasing sales by 20% over the next month. Achievable goals keep you motivated and stop you being frustrated.

R

Make sure your goal aligns with your bigger picture. If your focus is scaling your business when you're not live, a relevant goal might be to grow your email list by 25% using advertising. Keep your goals tied to your live selling journey and how far you want your business to grow.

T

Every goal needs a deadline. Setting a time frame keeps you accountable and stops you procrastinating. For example, "I want to reach 500 followers through live streams within the next three months" gives you a clear timeline to work toward.

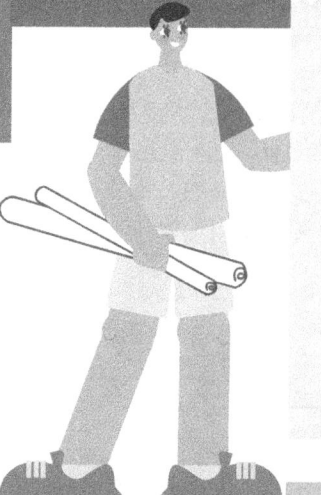

WHY NOT CREATE AND SELL YOUR OWN PRODUCTS?

Sometimes, the product you really want to sell can't be found on any supplier website. Because sometimes, the perfect product doesn't exist yet and is just waiting for you to create it.

Creative freedom, higher profits and standing out in the market. These are just some of the benefits you get when you make and sell your own products. On the flip side, creating, producing and marketing your products takes a ton of time, money and work.

So, is it worth it? You bet.

In today's world, creating a product is easier than ever before. If you don't have the skills to make something physical or digital, there are many tools out there that'll help you make something valuable from scratch. You can also use software to handle production, inventory and logistics.

And now that you're on your way to becoming a live selling big shot, you can sell your products through your live shopping sessions, cutting out the middleman.

You also benefit from having real-time feedback from your audience. It shows how your product scores on quality and fit. Analytics, too, help you spot what's working and what's not, letting you make quick fixes and keeping your products top-notch and in demand.

Here's how to go about creating your own products

1. Decide on Your Product — Develop an idea for a product, which can be anything from a physical good to a digital service

2. Make a Budget — How much will it cost to make? Ensure bringing your product into existence isn't going to break the bank.

3. Design Your Product — Depends on your product. You can design it yourself or hire a freelancer or company.

4. Get a Prototype — Put your product through its paces and make changes if needed. This saves you a ton of money from buying a full batch.

5. Test Your Product — Send your product out for reviews. Gather feedback and improve the product.

6. Set a Price & Market it — Take the amount it costs to produce and market your product, then add a percentage as a markup.

PRODUCT IDEAS TO CREATE OR HAVE MADE

- Handmade Crafts (jewelry, art, pottery, candles)
- Digital Products (eBooks, online courses, art prints)
- Fashion (scarfs, hats, bags, custom outfits)
- Personalized gifts (embroidered & engraved products)
- Print on demand (clothing, books, 3D printed goods)

AI, AR AND VR: LIVE SHOPPING
BEYOND REALITY

Artificial Intelligence (AI), Augmented Reality (AR) and Virtual Reality (VR) are shaking up the world! And as luck would have it, these high-tech tools are absolutely perfect for the world of live shopping.

Here's how they can be used to help you connect with your audience on a whole other level, making your streams more engaging, personal and fun than ever!

AI: PERSONALIZED MARKETING AT SCALE

AI is making ecommerce smarter, more personal and more efficient. Here's how:

- AI can look at lots of data to guess what customers might want or do next.
- Chatbots can talk to viewers right away, answering questions and helping with purchases.
- AI tools can make content, so you always have something interesting and relevant to share.

AR: ENHANCING VIEWER INTERACTION

AR makes shopping more enjoyable, adding digital fun to the real world:

- Viewers can see products in their space before buying, like placing virtual furniture in their room.
- AR can make your ads fun and interactive.
- Let your viewers try on clothes and makeup virtually, without leaving their homes.

VR: FULLY IMMERSIVE EXPERIENCES

VR is a major game changer, making viewers feel like they're shopping in store and holding products.

- Imagine setting up 3D spaces to let viewers explore clothes, jewelry, crafts and more items up close.
- Transport your audience to different locations or scenarios.
- VR can help demonstrate how your products work, showing buyers the features in an exciting and memorable way.

204 | THE ROAD AHEAD
LIVE SHOPPING
TOP TRENDS

Thanks to live shopping, ecommerce is entering a new era of growth and innovation. It's an exciting time for you to be getting started because you'll be among the early adopters embracing the technologies and strategies that'll define the future of online retail.

To help you navigate what's next for live selling, I've rounded up some of the top predicted ecommerce trends set to make an impact in the very near future.

12 PREDICTED TRENDS AND DEVELOPMENTS

An obvious one but **live shopping** is only gonna get bigger. That's why platforms like TikTok Live are all-in, and why I think Facebook will bring it back very soon.

AI avatars mean you don't need a well-groomed host. They almost perfectly mimic human actions with natural movements and expressions.

Having **AI Agents** run the show and manage video content and support in the background, means live shopping can run seamlessly **24/7**.

Smart speakers are seeing serious growth. More than 30% of US homes now own one. That means millions of people are buying stuff totally hands free.

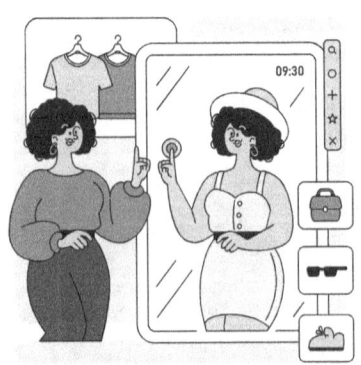

AR "**try before you buy without leaving your house**" will get even more sophisticated, saving us all from awkward returns.

THE ROAD AHEAD | 205

Gen Z and Millennials are all about **sustainability**. Most say it's a must for products they buy. Expect brands to produce more eco-friendly products to win more hearts and wallets.

Product **subscriptions** are a growing market. Perks like discounts and loyalty programs keep subscribers coming back.

We're glued to our phones. And with **responsive sites** and **one-click buying** making it all super easy, mobile shopping will become the norm.

As more and more people shop from their mobile, it'll become way easier to **buy while scrolling** their social media platforms.

Today's **AI chatbots** are practically human. They help you find, recommend and even buy stuff, making online shopping way less painful.

Blockchain is basically a digital diary that can't be tampered with. More brands will use it to secure payments, stop fraud and build trust with shoppers.

Shopping will become more personalized and seamless thanks to **big data** helping brands *get* you.

Data-driven recommendations mean you're more likely to buy products you'll truly love, meaning less impulse buys you'll toss out without ever using.

FAQs

How much does live selling cost?

It can be totally free if you have a smartphone and a dropshipping or "on demand" sales model that charges commission from purchases. This will only get you so far, though, and you'll need to level up your gear, software, marketing, support team and sales model if you want to scale up your business and earn more. Scale up slowly, prioritizing where to spend money that'll give you the greatest return on investment at each stage.

How long do my live events have to run for?

For as long as you like. And you can cut events short or run over, it's totally up to you and how you feel the event is going. Just keep your viewers informed along the way. You'd only need to worry about event length if you're using tools, equipment or something else that you pay for by time.

How often should I organize live events?

It's up to you. You can schedule a live event every day if you have the stamina for it. Every week is usually a good starting point, and you can add more days later. Once a month is probably not regular enough to build an engaging community of regular viewers.

Can I see and hear viewers during a live event?

Yes and no. Live selling is all about interactivity. On most platforms, your viewers will join events with their cam and mic turned off and type chat messages to communicate with you. You can then call out individual viewers by name to respond to their comments.

What is the best platform for live selling?

There's no one-size-fits-all for live selling. Different platforms attract different audiences, and with every example of successful and unsuccessful live sellers on one platform, there's an example of each on another platform. The best advice is to use the platform on which you already have a following.

How many followers do I need to start live selling?

Some platforms do have strict rules over minimum follower numbers before they'll let you go live. TikTok, for example, says you need at least 1,000 followers on the app before you can live stream. But even without these rules, you'll still be better off finding ways of increasing your follower count before you think about live selling.

How can I compete with so many others doing live selling?

Live selling is crowded, and more people are jumping on this new opportunity, but that just means there's proof it works. Rather than competitors, think of other live sellers as people to learn from and potentially even collaborate with. Focus on being yourself and building your community, and success will come. It's never as quick as any of us would like but it will come.

Do I have to complete KYC verification for all of my viewers?

No. Your platform will use a "Know Your Customer" (KYC) process to verify identities and ensure compliance with regulations in your region. But all platforms also enforce product compliance standards, meaning you must ensure your products meet local regulations. Contact your platform's support team if you're concerned about compliance.

GLOSSARY
WHAT THINGS MEAN

Brand: The concept that helps people recognize and identify a business or product.

Branding: The process of creating and maintaining your brand's image through visuals, messaging and experiences.

Collaborate: Working together with others to create, share or achieve something awesome.

Contingency: A backup plan for when things don't go quite as expected. You know, Murphy's Law stuff!

Cross-selling: Suggesting related products or services to your viewers to complement their original purchase.

Ecommerce: Buying and selling products online.

Engagement: The connection and interaction you build with your viewers, keeping them interested and involved.

Event: A planned livestream to connect with your viewers and showcase your products.

FOMO: Fear of Missing Out. A powerful feeling that makes people want to join in before it's too late.

Fulfillment: The process of packing and delivering orders to your viewers.

Giveaway: A fun way to attract attention and share your products by giving something away for free.

Home Shopping: Buying products from the comfort of your own home by watching live product demonstrations on TV.

Host: The person leading the live event, keeping the energy up and the audience engaged.

Influencer: Someone with a big following who can sway opinions or boost interest in your products.

Interaction: The back-and-forth moments when you and your viewers engage and connect.

Inventory: The stock of products you have ready to sell. Your treasure trove!

GLOSSARY | 209

Live Shopping: Real-time selling where viewers can shop while watching your stream.

Livestream: Broadcasting live video online to share and connect in the moment.

Loyalty: The trust and commitment your viewers show by coming back again and again.

Metrics: The numbers that measure your performance, helping you see what's working and what's not.

Moderate: Managing chats and interactions during a live event to keep things smooth and positive.

Niche: A specific segment of the market that your product or service serves. Your sweet spot!

Platform: The place where you host your live events or share your content, like YouTube, Facebook or TikTok.

Reach: The number of viewers your message or content can potentially connect with.

Script: A plan or outline for what you'll say during your event, keeping you organized and on track.

Segment: A group of people with shared traits in your audience.

Subscriber: Someone who's opted in to follow your updates, videos or emails.

Supplier: The person or business that provides the products you sell.

Timeline: The schedule or sequence of events to keep everything running smoothly and on time.

Transition: A shift between product demonstrations, segments or visuals during your live event.

Upselling: Offering premium or upgraded options to your viewers to maximize their experience.

Viewer: Someone tuning into your live event. Your audience and potential buyer.

BOOKMAP

DAY	TOPIC	PAGE
IT AIN'T YOUR GRANDMA'S QVC!		
-	LIVE SELLING: HOW IT WORKS	14
-	SHOPPING IN YOUR SLIPPERS	16
-	EAST VS WEST FROM CHINA TO THE WORLD	18
-	BIG BRANDS OR SOLO STARS	20
GEARING UP FOR THE JOURNEY		
1	SETTING UP YOUR STAGE	24
1	THE ESSENTIAL EQUIPMENT	26
1	SOME OTHER GEAR YOU MIGHT NEED	28
1	A BEGINNER'S GUIDE TO LIGHTING	30
1	LIGHTING YOUR STAGE	32
2	PICKING YOUR PLATFORM	34
2	BOOST ENTERTAINMENT WITH SOFTWARE & APPS	36
2	HOW TO GET & KEEP YOUR SELLER ACCOUNT	38
2	CREATING & OPTIMIZING YOUR SELLER ACCOUNT	40
3	CHOOSING A PROFITABLE NICHE	42
3	IDENTIFYING YOUR TARGET AUDIENCE	44
3	SOURCING YOUR PRODUCTS	46
3	BUILD RELATIONSHIPS WITH SUPPLIERS & VENDORS	48
3	HOW TO NEGOTIATE PRICES & TERMS	50
3	A WORD ABOUT LUXURY BRANDS	52
4	ORDER PROCESSING & FULFILLMENT SYSTEM	54
4	CALCULATING YOUR COSTS	56
4	COMPETITIVE PRICING FOR PROFIT	58
4	CRAFTING IRRESISTIBLE DEALS	60

BOOKMAP | 211

Section	DAY	TOPIC	PAGE
GEARING UP FOR THE JOURNEY	5	YOUR USP: WHAT SETS YOU APART?	62
		CRAFTING YOUR BRAND IDENTITY	64
		DESIGNING YOUR BRAND'S VISUAL (& AUDIO) ELEMENTS	66
PREPPING FOR THE SPOTLIGHT	6	DESIGN YOUR SHOW'S DNA	72
		PERFECTING YOUR SHOW TIMELINE	74
		EFFECTIVE PRODUCT DEMOS: UNBOXING	76
		EFFECTIVE PRODUCT DEMOS: IN ACTION	77
		HOW TO TALK ABOUT PRODUCTS	78
	7	OVERCOMING CAMERA SHYNESS	80
		DEVELOPING YOUR HOSTING PERSONA	82
		SPEAK WITH YOUR WHOLE SELF	84
	8	RESPONDING TO COMMENTS & QUESTIONS IN REAL-TIME	86
		MAKING YOUR AUDIENCE A COMMUNITY	88
		IDEAS TO KEEP YOUR LIVE EVENTS FRESH & FUN	90
	9	RUNNING AN EQUIPMENT SITE TEST	92
		HANDLING TECHNICAL PROBLEMS	94
		PRACTICING TRANSITIONS IN DEMOS	96
	10	GUESS WHAT? YOU'RE GOING LIVE TOMORROW!	98
		INVITE YOUR FRIENDS & FAMILY	100
GOING LIVE	11	PRE-SHOW CHECKLIST	106
		ENJOYING YOUR FIRST LIVE SALE	108
		POST-SHOW ANALYSIS & LESSONS LEARNED	110
SHIP ORDERS & ANALYSIS	12	PROCESSING YOUR FIRST ORDERS	116
		HANDLING SHIPPING & RETURNS	118
		GAIN VIEWER LOYALTY WITH GREAT SERVICE	120
	13	TRACKING THE KEY METRICS	122
		FINDING YOUR EDGE WITH ANALYTICS TOOLS	124

BOOKMAP

DAY	TOPIC	PAGE
14	HOW TO USE A/B TESTING	130
	INTRODUCING NEW PRODUCTS ON DEMAND	132
	INTRODUCING CROSS-SELL & UPSELL	134
	INTRODUCING PRODUCT BUNDLES	135
	RUNNING CONTESTS & GIVEAWAYS	136
	STRATEGIES FOR REWARDING LOYALTY	138
15	COLLABORATING WITH INFLUENCERS	140
	COLLABORATING WITH BRANDS	141
	IN-PERSON & ONLINE INTERVIEWS	142
	STREAMLINE YOUR DAY, SUPERCHARGE YOUR OUTPUT	144
16	HIRE AND TRAIN A VIRTUAL ASSISTANT	146
	INTEGRATING LIVE INTO YOUR MARKETING ECOSYSTEM SEAMLESSLY	148
	A VERY BRIEF GUIDE TO EMAIL MARKETING	150
17	THE MAGIC OF BEING REAL	156
	GRABBING ATTENTION LIKE A PRO	158
	HOW TO HANDLE OBJECTIONS	160
18	SCARCITY TACTICS. AKA FOMO	162
	LIMITED-TIME OFFERS & FLASH SALES	164
	ADDING COUNTDOWN TIMERS TO YOUR LIVESTREAM	166
	LEVERAGING SOCIAL PROOF	168
19	LEVERAGING SOCIAL PROOF: CRUSH IT IN STREAMS	170
	LEVERAGING SOCIAL PROOF: CRUSH IT ELSEWHERE	172
20	IDENTIFYING YOUR BEST TIMES TO STREAM	174
	PLANNING A THEME FOR A STREAM	176
	MAXIMIZING SALES IN THE SEASONS	178

SCALING YOUR OPERATIONS (Days 14–16)

PERFECTING YOUR CRAFT (Days 17–20)

BOOKMAP

Section	DAY	TOPIC	PAGE
LIGHTS, CAMERA, CHA-CHING!	21	PRE-EVENT MARKETING BLITZ	184
		IN-EVENT TACTICS FOR MAXIMIZING SALES	185
		PUTTING ALL THE PIECES TOGETHER FOR A HIGH-EARNING LIVE EVENT	186
		YOUR FIRST SALE$ LIVESTREAM	188
THE ROAD AHEAD	-	REFLECTING ON YOUR 21-DAY JOURNEY	194
		WHAT DO YOU DO WHEN YOU WANNA QUIT?	196
		SETTING NEW GOALS & SCALING UP	198
		WHY NOT CREATE AND SELL YOUR OWN PRODUCTS?	200
		AI, AR AND VR: LIVE SHOPPING BEYOND REALITY	202
		LIVE SHOPPING TOP TRENDS	204
	-	FAQS	206
		GLOSSARY	208
		BOOKMAP	210

www.ingramcontent.com/pod-product-compliance
Lightning Source LLC
LaVergne TN
LVHW012044070526
838202LV00056B/5585